USAF Southeast Asia Monograph Series
Volume V
Monograph 7

Airpower and the Airlift Evacuation of Kham Duc

Lieutenant Colonel Alan L. Gropman

New Imprint by
OFFICE OF AIR FORCE HISTORY
UNITED STATES AIR FORCE
WASHINGTON, D.C., 1985

Library of Congress Cataloging-in-Publication Data

Gropman, Alan L., 1938–
    Airpower and the airlift evacuation of Kham Duc.

    (USAF Southeast Asia monograph series; v. 5, monograph 7)
    Reprint. Originally published: Washington, D.C.: U.S. GPO, 1979.
    Bibliography: p. 85.
    1. Vietnamese Conflict, 1961–1975—Aerial operations, American. 2. Airlift, Military. I.
Title. II. Series.
DS558.8.G76 1986   959.704′348   85–18905

This volume is a reprint of a 1976 edition originally issued by the Air University.

ISBN: 978-1-78039-297-4

For sale by the Superintendent of Documents, U.S. Government Printing Office
Washington, D.C., 20402

Foreword

THIS slender volume has value for both the general reader and the aviation specialist. For the latter there are lessons regarding command and control and combined-unit operations that need to be learned to achieve battlefield success. For the former there is a straightforward narrative about American aviators of all four services struggling in the most difficult of conditions to try to rescue more than 1,500 American and Vietnamese military and civilians. Not all the Americans moving through the events recounted in this monograph acted heroically, but most did, and it was their heroism that gave the evacuation the success it had.

Airpower and the Airlift Evacuation of Kham Duc is fully documented so that readers wishing to look deeper into this incident may do so. Those who study the battle will see that it was something of a microcosm of the entire Vietnam War in the relationship of airpower to tactical ground efforts. Kham Duc sat at the bottom of a small green mountain bowl, and during most of 12 May 1968 the sky was full of helicopters, forward air controller aircraft, transports, and fighters, all striving to succeed and to avoid running into each other in what were most trying circumstances. In the end they carried the day, though by the narrowest of margins and with heavy losses.

RAYMOND B. FURLONG
Lieutenant General, USAF
Commander, Air University

Acknowledgments

I was especially blessed on this project with thoroughly warm interest from numerous people. All historians depend utterly on archivists, and those from the Alfred F. Simpson Historical Research Center were especially cooperative. Three of the many stand out—Judy Endicott, Wayne Robinson, and Kathy Nichols were as eager to tell of the evacuation from Kham Duc as I was. The narrative before the reader would have been incomplete without help from numerous officers and enlisted men who gave their time for interviews or writing letters. Their names can be found in the bibliography. Likewise, the monograph would have been empty without the fine photographs supplied by the Air Force Audiovisual Service, and the many others supplied by participants in the evacuation. I was also helped by several skillful and interested editors who sanded the rough spots off the manuscript. Robert Bogard, John Schlight, and Glenn Morton spent many hours making intelligible syntax of my drafts. I am especially grateful for the encouragement I received from Donaldson Frizzell, who helped me conceive of this school project as a publishable monograph. I was also greatly aided by my wife, Jackie, who supported me throughout by reading and criticizing preliminary drafts, and by my daughter, Beth, who did likewise. They took a special interest in Kham Duc because they knew some of the principals and, with my elder son, Mike, waited for me in 1968 and 1969 while I flew in Vietnam.

ALAN L. GROPMAN
Lieutenant Colonel, USAF

Biographical Sketch

Lieutenant Colonel Alan L. Gropman (PhD, Tufts University) has been a long-time student of military history. His interest in the evacuation of Kham Duc was born of his many years as a C-130 navigator, the loss of several friends during the evacuation, and his long friendship with one of the last men rescued. He is a graduate of Squadron Officer School, Air Command and Staff College (nonresident seminar), the Industrial College of the Armed Forces (correspondence), and the Air War College, class of 1978. He has served as a branch chief in the Directorate of Operations, Headquarters United States Air Forces in Europe, and a Section Chief in the Directorate of Plans at Headquarters Air Force.

Abstract

TITLE: Airpower and the Airlift Evacuation of Kham Duc

AUTHOR: Alan L. Gropman, Lt Colonel, USAF

This narrative describes the evacuation of more than 1,400 American soldiers, Marines, and airmen, and Vietnamese men, women, and children from the Kham Duc Special Forces camp in southern I Corps on 12 May 1968. It treats the geographical and topographical setting, the threat to the camp posed by two regiments of the North Vietnamese Army, and the danger to the camp and its inhabitants from the communist seizure of all the high ground around the camp. The monograph devotes individual chapters to the US Army and Marine helicopter rescue efforts, tactical air support, and tactical airlift. The final chapter deals with the attempts to rescue the last three men at Kham Duc. American aircraft losses were severe during the evacuation, and the successful outcome of the mass rescue depended upon the skill and courage of American aircrews. Had command and control been better, losses probably would have been less severe.

Table of Contents

"...TO ALL WHO SERVED"

CHAPTER I

The Setting

INTRODUCTION

The US Army Special Forces camp at Kham Duc was attacked by the army of North Vietnam and evacuated by combined American arms in the spring of 1968. That year is now seen as a climacteric in the Vietnam war. Near the end of January 1968, during the Tet holiday truce, the Viet Cong and North Vietnamese army, in violation of that truce, attacked Saigon and all 34 provincial capitals, as well as numerous cities, towns, villages, and military installations throughout South Vietnam. Because they struck while most of the South Vietnamese military were on leave, the communists achieved initial surprise and temporary, major gains. The offensive, which began in late January, was sustained for several weeks in most of the country and for several months in those parts of South Vietnam nearest enemy sanctuaries in Laos and Cambodia. During this period, the Marine base at Khe Sanh, in northern I Corps (the most northern military district in South Vietnam), came under heavy attack and was besieged from late January until the first week in April. Even after the siege was broken on 6 April, Khe Sanh suffered daily artillery attacks from the communists in the hills around it. The siege, which was part of the most powerfully coordinated enemy offensive of the war until that date and for six years to come, was broken by a nearly unprecedented display of airpower. US Air Force, Navy, and Marine fighters dropped 40,000 tons of bombs on communist positions, while USAF B-52s bombed enemy concentrations with 60,000 tons of ordnance. The USAF para-dropped 12,000 tons of supplies into Khe Sanh to sustain it during the siege while the camp was under constant enemy shelling and probing attacks. Defenders on the ground fired 200,000 artillery and mortar rounds at their attackers to keep them at bay. Most of these shells had been air dropped to them.[1] Similarly, airpower permitted the successful evacuation of Kham Duc when it was surrounded and assaulted barely a month after the siege of Khe Sanh was lifted.

GEOGRAPHY AND TOPOGRAPHY

The camp at Kham Duc was named for a small village 800 meters from its defense compound. It was situated south of Khe Sanh but also in I Corps, in the northern section of Quang Tin province, about 75 miles west of Tam Ky and the coast and only 10 miles from Laos (see Appendix B). The camp was located about mid-way along a 6,000-foot asphalt runway, both of which were dominated by steeply rising terrain in all directions. Making an approach into the airstrip resembled flying into a green bowl with the field at the bottom. The hills were densely forested with double and triple jungle canopy. It was obvious to those on the ground at Kham Duc and to the aircrews who flew into the airfield that the strip and camp were vulnerable to an enemy in the surrounding high ground.[2] (see Appendix C)

Kham Duc sat beside national highway 14, which paralleled the Laotian border and had served as an avenue for insurgents to move from Laos north and east to the coastal plain around Da Nang. The camp contained a strike force which had several missions: interdiction of enemy lines of communication in the region, of which the main one was highway 14; control of population and resources in that part of I Corps; reconnaissance of enemy movements; combat operations; and training of Civilian Irregular Defense Group (CIDG) personnel. There were few civilians in the immediate area because the only village was Kham Duc, and 85 percent of its 272 inhabitants were civilian dependents of the camp's Vietnamese strike force. Since April 1968, US Army engineer units had been working at the camp to build a hard surface base for a radio navigation facility, make runway repairs, and construct general camp improvements. After the fall of Lang Vei (between Kham Duc and Khe Sanh) in February during the height of the Tet offensive, Kham Duc had been the only border surveillance camp remaining in I Corps.[3] Perhaps because of its excellent location to monitor and

Kham Duc Airfield. This photograph was taken from the southeast of the runway looking north. The field sat at the bottom of a green bowl with steeply rising terrain in all directions.

Kham Duc Special Forces Camp. The photograph was taken looking west from a point slightly outside the camp perimeter. Note the parking and offloading ramp in the center of the photograph.

interdict enemy operations and the signs that the Americans were upgrading the base, Kham Duc was singled out for a major attack. Its vulnerability to fire from the surrounding hills was probably another factor.

REINFORCEMENT OF KHAM DUC

In early April 1968, intelligence analysts began to observe signs that Kham Duc was threatened. On the 5th and 12th of that month the camp was identified as being under a significant threat, and on the 19th and 26th large enemy concentrations were reported in the region. The Viet Cong and North Vietnamese were known to be building roads in the area, one of which connected their road system in Laos with highway 14 south of Kham Duc. On 3 May, large enemy forces were again reported in the camp's area, and shortly thereafter a captured insurgent revealed that his unit was scheduled to attack Kham Duc.[4]

Because of the threat to this uniquely situated camp, Military Assistance Command, Vietnam (MACV), directed Kham Duc's reinforcement and ordered a battalion task force of troops from the Americal Division into the camp. On 10 May, more than 600 troops and some supporting artillery and ammunition were brought into Kham Duc, and an additional 32 troops and more supplies were flown in on 11 May. The men, equipment and ammunition were carried in on C-130s flying under a tactical emergency

3

Reinforcement of Kham Duc. C-130 mission to Kham Duc in April 1968 during the period when Army engineers were building and repairing the camp and facilities. Note ridge to the immediate north of the runway: enemy gunners occupied it during 12 May. Also note Army engineering equipment on west side of runway.

priority, the highest airlift category in Vietnam, and all had been diverted from other missions, actions underscoring the awareness that Kham Duc was under imminent threat. The Americal battalion about doubled the fighting force at Kham Duc. Late in the day on 10 May there were reported to be 1,760 people at Kham Duc; 272 of these were Vietnamese dependents, and the remainder were American Army, Marine, and Air Force soldiers, engineers, and advisors and Vietnamese CIDG troops.[5]

The emergency seemed to be highlighted by the mortar fire which bracketed the C-130 that brought into Kham Duc Lt Col Robert B. Nelson, commander of the Second Battalion, 1st Infantry, 196th Infantry Brigade. He set to work immediately with his men preparing a defense perimeter and tying it into the defenses already built by the Special Forces, their indigenous allies, and the Army engineers.[6] Colonel Nelson must have known that he was in for a fight to preserve Kham Duc's excellent tactical location, because when he departed Hue Phu Bai in northern I Corps for the camp to the south, he refused to take with him on the mission any men with less than 60 days remaining on their tour in Vietnam.[7]

THE FALL OF NGOC TAVAK

As Colonel Nelson and his men were arriving at Kham Duc with reinforcements, the camp's main forward operating base, Ngoc Tavak, was

4

Americal Division artillery fires into the hills surrounding Kham Duc. Photo taken in 1970 after Kham Duc was reoccupied.

105 mm howitzer pointed at the hills surrounding Kham Duc. Photo taken in 1970 after Kham Duc was reoccupied.

being overrun by two North Vietnamese regiments. This post was three miles southwest of Kham Duc and was located at the site of an old French fort. It also had an airstrip, although much shorter than Kham Duc's, and the camp and strip were also dominated by the high terrain around them. Ngoc Tavak had been under mounting artillery pressure and ground probes since 6 May and was running low on ammunition. The base's function was to expand the border surveillance and patrolling efforts from the main camp at Kham Duc, especially along highway 14 (which was in view of Ngoc Tavak). The base had been established because patrols from Kham Duc had most frequently sighted enemy troops in this area.[8]

At Ngoc Tavak there were 33 US Marines, 8 US Army Special Forces troops, 3 Australian advisors, and 173 CIDG soldiers. On 9 May, after four days of constant artillery bombardment and fighting off enemy troops on the defensive wire of the camp's compound, the CIDG forces elected, against the advice of the Americans, to try to move back to Kham Duc along highway 14. They were ambushed by a dug-in enemy between Ngoc Tavak and Kham Duc, and those who survived the attack returned to Ngoc Tavak. Early on the morning of 10 May, the communists attacked with a heavy mortar and artillery barrage, following up with a heavy ground attack. During the ground battle some unidentified Vietnamese troops approached the Marine section of the compound shouting: "Don't shoot, don't shoot, friendly, friendly," but as they got within close range, these men unleashed a grenade, satchel charge, and small arms attack on the Marines, inflicting heavy casualties. The defenders noted that some of the incoming small arms fire was from carbines—which was the type of weapon used by their CIDG forces. Since all of the dead North Vietnamese army troops were carrying new AK-47 rifles, the Americans made the presumption that some of the camp's indigenous defenders had turned on them.[9] True or not, since more than 80 percent of the base's fighting force was irregular Vietnamese, this presumption upset the Americans.

Another cause for concern among the Americans was their small amount of artillery and inadequate stock of ammunition. The base had only two 105 mm howitzers and four mortars of assorted sizes for artillery. On 10 May the American contingent fired the last 100 rounds of artillery in their defense and then disabled their weapons. Their survival during the last two days at the camp depended upon their rifles and the air support they received from an AC-47 gunship and tactical fighter sorties controlled by a forward air controller (FAC). AC-47 (Spooky) gunships had been overhead Ngoc Tavak for several days, and the aircrews had used their machine guns to break up attacks and enemy concentrations. On 10 May, they killed numerous enemy soldiers who had captured sections of the base. Sometimes the gunships were directed to fire on parts of the base that had been overrun, even when the defenders believed that friendly wounded were still in that part of the compound.[10] The situation had become that desperate.

USAF AC-47, "Spooky," gunship similar to those that supported Ngoc Tavak in its final four days.

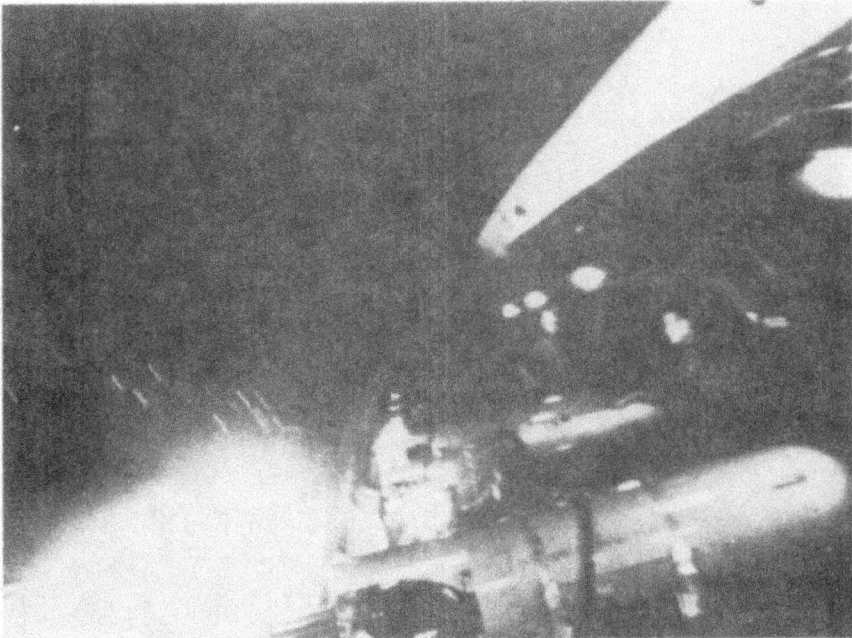

AC-47 gunships, three 7.62 mm miniguns. These guns fired at the rate of 100 rounds per second.

Late in the day a small contingent of reinforcements arrived in four Marine CH-46 helicopters, but the last two aircraft received ground fire, and both were lost on the landing strip at Ngoc Tavak. Not only did this demonstrate the Communist domination of the strip, the downed aircraft almost completely blocked it for further use. Soon after, all but out of ammunition, and with two helicopters on fire on the landing strip, the men were ordered to destroy the rest of their equipment and withdraw to Kham Duc. A small medical evacuation helicopter was sent in from Kham Duc to remove the seriously wounded, but indigenous forces rushed onto it, preventing the removal of those who most needed it. As the overloaded helicopter took off, several CIDG troops held onto the skids, only to fall off or be shot off high over the jungle.[11]

After destroying the rest of their equipment with a claymore mine, the men, assisted by fighter strikes, left the camp for Kham Duc. Because of the ambush of the CIDG forces the previous day, the American and Vietnamese troops left the base in a southeasterly direction, crossed the Dak So River, avoided all open areas, climbed a hill a mile from their abandoned fort, and hacked out of the jungle a landing zone for helicopters. They were picked up by four CH-46 helicopters that made several shuttles each, and all the survivors were back at the main camp by 1900 on 10 May.[12] Losses had been heavy: 15 Americans killed (one US Army and 14 Marines); 52 defenders wounded (two Army, 21 Marines, 29 CIDG); and 64 troops missing in action

Marine CH-46 helicopter similar to those used to rescue the forces at Ngoc Tavak. Two CH-46s were lost on 10 May.

Army UH-1 helicopter similar to the one sent to rescue the wounded at Ngoc Tavak on 10 May.

(of which two were US Army and the remainder CIDG). Those who were seriously wounded were flown out of Kham Duc on 11 May by USAF C-7A aircraft.[13] Those not fortunate enough to be evacuated on 11 May faced a very heavy attack at Kham Duc on 12 May and experienced their second evacuation in two days, as the communist force that had attacked them moved the three miles north from Ngoc Tavak to the main camp at Kham Duc, forcing its abandonment.[14]

THE DECISION TO EVACUATE KHAM DUC

The main camp had been subject to intensifying artillery, mortar and recoilless rifle attacks throughout 10 and 11 May, but because there had been no extensive ground probes on those days, the defenders had an opportunity to tighten their defense perimeter. Despite Kham Duc's reinforcement, the defenses of the camp were thin, and the enemy had already secured positions in the high ground from which to pound the camp accurately. On 11 May, 30 B-52s dropped several hundred tons of bombs on suspected enemy positions between Ngoc Tavak and Kham Duc, but apparently this attack brought little relief.[15] Also on 11 May, Lt Gen Robert E. Cushman, Jr., Commander of the III Marine Amphibious Force (MAF), recommended to Gen William Westmoreland, Commander US Military Assistance Command, Vietnam (COMUSMACV), that Kham Duc be evacuated. Westmoreland ordered the camp's evacuation because it did not have the "defensive potential of Khe

USAF C-7A transport aircraft similar to those used to evacuate the wounded from Kham Duc on 11 May.

Sanh. . . ." He left the actual timing of the withdrawal to Maj Gen Samuel Koster, Commander of the American Division.[16] Before 0100 on the next day—12 May—the leaders of the Army Special Forces A Team received a message from higher headquarters that the camp would be evacuated later that day.[17] For some unknown reason some units in the camp, Americans as well as Vietnamese, were left uninformed of that decision until many hours later. As will be shown below, many Air Force personnel on the ground and overhead Kham Duc did not know of the decision made on 11 May to give up the camp until many hours after the decision had been made.

THE CAPTURE OF THE OPERATING POSTS

During the remaining hours of darkness, the pressure on the camp steadily rose. The US Army had placed machine guns in the mountains surrounding the camp to serve as advanced defensive positions. The communists prepared for their final assault on Kham Duc by attacking and capturing these outposts one at a time. Several fell before first light, and all had fallen soon after daybreak. There were seven such outposts surrounding the airstrip and camp. Outpost number 7 fell at 0423, and this was reported to I Corps Direct Air Support Center (I DASC), which scrambled fighters to the beleaguered camp.

Thirty minutes after the capture of outpost 7, outpost number 1 radioed the main camp that it was surrounded. Its defenders elected to burrow deeply into their bunker and called for the AC-47 Spooky gunship to fire directly into their outpost to break up the attack. This was done, and the communist attack was temporarily stopped. Soon thereafter, however, this post was also overrun, and its defenders escaped back to Kham Duc. Similarly, a half hour after Spooky fired directly into outpost 1, the defenders of outpost number 3 called on the Americal Division battalion artillery to zero in on their outpost and blast away their attackers.[18] Soon all seven outposts were in enemy hands. Observing the fall of each of these in succession deepened the sense of foreboding of Kham Duc's contingent because they could see on their charts, as they crossed off each outpost, the increasing enemy domination of the terrain around them. Not only could the communists, well covered by jungle canopy, fire down into the camp from advantageous positions, they could also fire down at support aircraft attempting to resupply the camp or to extract people from it.

EARLY DAYLIGHT ATTACKS

As the sun came up, ground fog formed, obscuring the movements of the communists in the high ground around the camp. The fog, which lasted several hours, also slowed down the ground probes slightly. An hour before the fog lifted, 24 additional B-52s dropped several hundred more tons of bombs on suspected enemy concentrations to the south of Kham Duc, but none of these bombs fell within three kilometers of the camp.[19] Given the unabated ferocity of the ground attack after the fog dissipated, this bombing raid seems to have had little positive effect. For at 0935, with the fog lifted,

USAF B-52, similar to those that bombed suspected enemy positions on 12 May.

the North Vietnamese regiments made a massive ground assault against the southeastern side of the compound, having used fog and terrain to mask their movement. A combination of artillery fired point blank at the enemy, tactical-fighter airstrikes, and small-arms fire broke up the attack, but before it ended, another attack had begun at the opposite end of the compound, further demonstrating that the enemy had surrounded the camp.[20] Later in the morning, the enemy could again be seen at the defensive wire which circled the camp, and it became increasingly tricky to kill the enemy with air attacks because of the proximity of the communists to friendly troops.[21]

As the pressure on the camp built, the resolve of the indigenous forces appeared to weaken, a fact which added to the apprehensions of the Americans. The rumor that some of the CIDG forces at Ngoc Tavak had apparently fired on and killed several Marines spread through the main camp on 10 and 11 May. On the 12th, elements of the CIDG force at Kham Duc refused to make a combat sweep of the rear of the camp when ordered to do so, and the local Vietnamese commander refused to leave his bunker to encourage his men. One Army Special Forces soldier reported that the "control of the CIDG was sorry as hell,"[22] and Special Forces A Team commander, Capt Robert Henderson, noted that one company of CIDG was never subjected to ground attack in their part of the compound and received only one or two mortar shells during the constant barrage.[23] Henderson obviously doubted their loyalty. One Army lieutenant recorded that the morale and discipline of the Vietnamese were poor and that some of the local forces left their assigned defensive positions without permission. To stop the indigenous forces from abandoning key posts and falling back on the runway, leaving the perimeter undefended, this lieutenant had to threaten to shoot anyone leaving his position.[24] Small wonder, then, that when Col. Claude H. Turner, the senior controller of the airborne Battlefield Command and Control Center (ABCCC), talked to Lieutenant Colonel Nelson, the battalion commander, Turner detected anxiety and "emotionalism" in Nelson's voice as he called for more assistance.[25]

DISASTER AT THE AIRSTRIP

On the airfield things seemed to be going from bad to worse. Around 0730 the first helicopter, an Army CH-47, arrived to evacuate people, but as it landed it took multiple hits, burst into flames and exploded, blocking the runway. The Army engineers sent a bulldozer to push the burning hulk off the runway, but the enemy disabled the bulldozer and killed the driver as he reached the burning helicopter, adding to the obstacles preventing fixed wing aircraft from using the strip. Nearly simultaneously, an Air Force A-1E fighter plane was shot down outside the camp perimeter.[26]

It took more than an hour to clear the runway, and soon after it was cleared, a C-130, heavy with supplies, landed. Just before touchdown, ground fire punctured one of its main landing gear tires and the main wing fuel tanks. When the crew opened the ramp to discharge cargo, the plane was

USAF B-52s, similar to those employed at Kham Duc on 12 May, bombing suspected enemy positions in South Viet Nam.

Army CH-47 helicopter (hovering), similar to the one lost early in the morning of 12 May at Kham Duc.

rushed by Vietnamese women, children, and some CIDG troops, who ran without any order or discipline into the partly emptied cargo compartment. Some of the women and children were elbowed out of the way and trampled by CIDG troops anxious to escape Kham Duc. The Vietnamese on the airplane packed themselves against the remaining cargo and could not be moved off the floor and out of the airplane so that the loadmaster could empty it. The aircraft commander decided to try to evacuate the Vietnamese from Kham Duc but because the C-130 had a flat tire, and was heavy with cargo and the additional load of passengers, he was unable to accelerate to takeoff speed on a partly blocked runway pockmarked and littered with debris. After the pilot turned around and taxied off the runway, the passengers became suddenly movable as they realized that a parked C-130 was an inviting target for communist gunners in the hills.[27]

The evacuation had an inauspicious beginning: the enemy crippled the first two aircraft to land, shot down a fighter, and demonstrated their complete domination of the field. In some cases the enemy was using 50-caliber machine guns that the defenders of the outposts had abandoned in their haste to return to Kham Duc.[28] The news of the aircraft losses soon reached MACV, and the headquarters advised the troops in the camp that there would be no more C-130 missions to Kham Duc because of the danger caused by the intense ground fire.[29] Once that fact became general knowledge, no one in the camp doubted that their survival depended upon tactical air support.

The successful, sustained defense of the camp for the next several hours, until fixed-wing evacuation could begin, was brought about by the repeated attacks from the air, most of which were supplied by the USAF. The

USAF C-130, similar to the one damaged at Kham Duc early on 12 May.

USAF A-1E piston driven fighter airplane, similar to the aircraft shot down at Kham Duc early in the morning of 12 May.

successful extraction of the vast majority of the camp defenders and Vietnamese dependents was a costly venture. Seven US aircraft were lost in about nine hours over Kham Duc: one CH-47, one A-1E, one USMC CH-46, one Army UH-1C, one USAF 0-2; and two C-130s. The Marines also lost two CH-46s at Ngoc Tavak on 10 May.

On 12 May, in addition to the AC-47 gunship sorties and B-52 strikes, there was a C-130 airdrop of ammunition and more than 120 USAF and 16 Marine fighter sorties, as well as many Army helicopter gunship sorties.[30] But for all of the air support, the margin of victory was narrow—in that the people were extracted just before the camp fell—and the losses were stiff. In addition to the seven airplanes, all heavy equipment was abandoned, including all engineering equipment and the 105 mm howitzers, which were destroyed in the final minutes. There were 25 Americans killed, 96 wounded, and 64 missing, and the Vietnamese took several hundred casualties.[31] Of the 1,760 at Kham Duc on 10 May, about 1,500 were returned to safety; the bulk of the missing were 183 civilian Vietnamese,[32] most of whom were killed in a C-130 shot down in the late afternoon (see Chapter IV). Before the evacuation was completed at 1645, all people on the ground were airlifted out. Without the courage of the aircrews the losses would have been much higher, and possibly no one would have survived the onslaught at Kham Duc on 12 May 1968.

CHAPTER II

Marine and Army Helicopter Support

INTRODUCTION

As in the case of Khe Sanh, by no means was all of the air support supplied by the Air Force. Although it is impossible to know the precise number of Marine and Army helicopter sorties at Kham Duc on 12 May, there were at least 41 Army CH-47 sorties and probably 30 Marine CH-46 sorties to evacuate the military and Vietnamese dependents. The Marine and Army helicopters, in fact, evacuated slightly more than half of the people on 12 May. There were, furthermore, at least 12 Army UH-1 sorties used for evacuation and rescue, and six Army helicopter gunships on station at various times during the day to suppress ground fire and to provide defensive fire support as needed for rescue missions and for other purposes. Unlike the jet fighters, which carried bombs and cannon, these helicopters carried heavy-caliber machine guns, had excellent loiter capabilities, and could concentrate on a hostile target for a much greater length of time than could the high-speed fighters. They were also much more vulnerable to ground fire.[1] As the ground fire intensified during the afternoon and there were fewer and fewer defenders on the ground to put up a fight in their own behalf, the number of helicopters diminished, and in the last minutes USAF tactical fighters helped the AF airlifters finish the evacuation.[2]

Because the Kham Duc force was unprepared for an emergency evacuation, and because there was no experience integrating the numbers and types of aircraft in such a small target area in such concentration, many of the procedures established during the day were improvised by the aircrews and aircrew leaders. Aircrew briefings were sketchy and incomplete in this ad hoc evacuation, and frequently crews arriving on the scene found that the briefings had not depicted the situation accurately or had left them with an incomplete knowledge of their mission.[3] Given, however, the speed with which the situation deteriorated and the distance of the various headquarters from the action (never less than 100 and some as much as 300 miles from Kham Duc), the weakness of the briefings should be weighed in the balance with the overwhelming amount of airpower brought to bear on the problem.

The lack of coordination and inadequate command and control were caused mainly by the "fog of war."

EARLY ARMY HELICOPTER MISSIONS

In any case, however well or poorly briefed, the pilot of the first CH-47 flying into Kham Duc was shot down, and his helicopter ended up blocking the runway. The stricken aircraft had been a part of a two-ship mission sent from Chu Lai Air Base (AB), home of the Americal Division. The crew of the second ship, observing the destruction of the first, broke off the approach to the field, orbited while trying to comprehend the situation; and left after 20 minutes to fly to a nearby helicopter landing zone (LZ) named LZ Ross. Here the crew awaited further instructions. About two hours later, at 1015, this aircraft, now a part of a four-ship flight, returned to the Kham Duc area. On this, his second sortie into the area, the pilot, now number four in the flight, was forced to break off his landing approach because of the intensity of the ground fire. After returning to LZ Ross for fuel, the aircrew tried again about two hours later. While enroute to the camp, the pilot was able to contact other aircrews returning from Kham Duc and became familiar with the best approaches into the camp and the location of the troops and dependents to be extracted. On this, the third attempt, with the weather deteriorating, the crew succeeded in landing and evacuated a helicopter-load of surrounded Americans and South Vietnamese.[4]

While this CH-47 was in orbit on the first approach into Kham Duc in the early morning, Army helicopter gunships were in the air providing support for the lightly armed UH-1, CH-47, and CH-46 evacuation helicopters. One of the gunship pilots who saw the first CH-47 try to land was quoted later as saying that the ground fire just "ate him up." As indicated in Chapter I, while the first CH-47 was being destroyed, an Air Force A-1E piston-driven fighter plane that had been dropping napalm and cluster bomb units (CBUs) on the ridge line above the camp was shot down. The pilot of the fighter plane was rescued by an Army pilot in a lightly armed UH-1 helicopter, while a pair of Army helicopter gunships provided fire support. The two gunships, already struck several times by ground fire, went into an orbit around the fighter pilot—who had bailed out and was receiving a great deal of enemy fire as he hung helplessly in his parachute—while a lightly armed UH-1 "Slick" helicopter pilot prepared to land and pick him up. The fire was so intense, in fact, that the gunship pilots were surprised that the parachuting pilot survived the attack. The gunship pilots were told to stay on station by the "Slick" pilot: "I'll go down and get him, I'll go down and get him; you follow me." The gunship pilots effectively suppressed the communist ground fire during the descent of the fighter pilot and the landing of their colleague in his helicopter. One gunship pilot estimated that there were two companies of North Vietnamese in the area of the downed A-1E pilot, and he reported that they were "just like ants down there, they'd stand behind trees and shoot at you, you just couldn't begin to kill them all." Immediately after the fighter pilot landed, the UH-1 pilot rushed up to him, cut the parachute shroud lines with his knife, dragged the fighter pilot over to his helicopter, threw him bodily into his craft, and took off to safety. On the way out of the Kham Duc area, the two gunships provided escort for the "Slick" and its human cargo. The gunship pilot likened the Kham Duc area to a World War II movie, with "burning airplanes all over hell." He and his comrades stayed on station for 45 minutes and took many hits. When they retired to the rear for refueling, they were refused permission to return to Kham Duc because of the battle damage to their helicopters and the growing intensity of the ground fire.[5]

Army UH-1 helicopters, similar to those used to rescue small loads of people at Kham Duc on 12 May and to the "Slick" piloted by Mr. Fitzsimmons who rescued the downed A-1E pilot.

Through their efforts they saved one A-1E pilot and provided the margin of safety for one of their own colleagues. Shortly thereafter one of the UH-1 helicopters was shot down, but the pilot, unlike that of the A-1E, was able to crash land (through auto-rotating) inside the camp perimeter and near the runway. His aircraft landed on its side and on fire, and, while he was trying to cut off the switches, he was literally pulled out the front window and pushed into a bunker by people on the ground. Minutes later mortar fire struck the helicopter.[6]

HELICOPTER COORDINATION EMERGES OVER KHAM DUC

Throughout the morning and into the afternoon, other helicopter crews evacuated people, while tactical fighter pilots bombed the enemy on the flight corridors into Kham Duc used by the Army and Marine helicopters.[7] Even at that, many helicopters were struck by ground fire. Beyond the

Army UH-1 armed helicopter similar to those employed at Kham Duc on 12 May.

Close-up of the UH-1 machine guns.

Army CH-47 helicopters similar to those employed at Kham Duc on 12 May.

Marine CH-46 helicopter, similar to those employed at Kham Duc on 12 May.

dangers of ground fire were dangerous airspace coordination problems. Since the operation had not been preplanned, there was no overall helicopter control to offer guidance and to direct the operation. An Air Force ABCCC had been on station since about 0900, but it was busy directing fighter strikes and tanker operations. The ABCCC, furthermore, had no experience with helicopters, and did not have the right radios for contacting most of them. Radio frequency coordination had long been a problem in combined operations in Vietnam, because not all the aircraft had all the radios used by all other aircraft.[8]

To remedy the helicopter control problem, one of the UH-1 pilots appointed himself director of helicopter operations at Kham Duc. The call sign of his aircraft was Arab 03, and when he departed the area for fuel, another helicopter pilot, in a CH-47 with the call sign Boxcar 23, took over. These two aircraft alternated directing operations until the last helicopter left in the afternoon. Arab 03 and Boxcar 23 told helicopter pilots which path to take into the camp, which tactics to use to minimize danger, how to obtain fighter support, and where to go to pick up evacuees. Boxcar 23 and Arab 03 were also similarly able to assist some of the Air Force transports. The tactic they most recommended was a high-speed dive into the camp, approaching from across the hills on the northwest side of Kham Duc and landing to the southeast.[9]

For all of the efforts of Arab 03 and Boxcar 23, however, there was still much confusion in the helicopter mission, because not all the aircraft entering the area had been briefed on the services offered by these two Army pilots. One Marine helicopter pilot complained that there was "no real coordination agency" at Kham Duc. When he arrived he thought he was on his own, and he was not able to contact anyone in the air, including the ABCCC, because his radios did not match those in the C-130 ABCCC over Kham Duc. He found the operation a "hit or miss situation of landing on the field and hoping these people were at the right location."[10] Other Marine

22

aircrews, by way of contrast, found Arab 03 and Boxcar 23 to be "natural born" leaders, who provided "outstanding" services and control.[11]

Although the alternating Army helicopters were able to assist many of the helicopter crews, they were not able to produce effective coordination between the high-speed tactical fighters and the helicopters, and neither was the ABCCC. Many of the helicopter aircrews, who were generous in their praise of Arab 03 and Boxcar 23, complained of the lack of information on fighter sweeps and of the general lack of intelligence and direction. One Marine element leader from Danang, who led four CH-46s into Kham Duc in the afternoon, did not know that he might be rescuing Vietnamese women and children—likely to be hysterical—and was not fully cognizant of the extreme danger to both the evacuees and himself until he arrived over the field, although he had become partly aware of the problem on the way inbound by talking to departing helicopter crews as they left Kham Duc. When he arrived he could see abundant Army CH-47s, seemingly everywhere, and many tactical fighters. He and his element orbited for a time while he tried many different radio frequencies in an attempt to contact somebody in control, but his efforts were fruitless. He finally raised the A Team leadership (who were using call sign Brassy Study). They told him that things were worsening and that he should bring in his element when he thought he had a good chance of succeeding. The leader took his group into the camp out of a high spiral and maneuvered to the west side of the runway, looking for the people Brassy Study said would be there. There were, however, no people lined up as advised. Instead there was a group of people some distance off in the middle of the landing strip, and, despite the mortar shells, the helicopters moved up to the American and Vietnamese soldiers and civilians and took out several groups. This four-ship element was able to make several shuttles, each time taking out nine people per aircraft.[12]

The helicopter crews did not let the lack of an advance plan for such an operation, nor the lack of coordination, nor the risk of colliding with other helicopters or fast moving fighters, nor the risks of being struck by intense ground fire get in their way. It was apparent to the aircrews that the people on the ground were in serious trouble, so they bitched about all of the confusion and complications but did the job professionally and rescued more than 700 people.

CHAPTER III

Tactical Air Support

INTRODUCTION

The firepower supplied by more than 140 tactical fighter sorties was the major factor that permitted the Army and Marine helicopters to save as many people as they did. Fighter support was also the reason the C-123s and C-130s were able to complete the extraction. Within minutes of the call for help from Kham Duc early in the morning of 12 May, I DASC was scrambling fighters to help the camp and gathering others for use during the day. Fighters were supplied by three United States services: the Navy, Marines, and Air Force; from two allies—the United States and Vietnam; and also by American forces stationed in Thailand. The Marines offered about 16 A-4D sorties, the Navy supplied at least two fighter sorties, the Vietnamese air force contributed at least six F-5 sorties, and the USAF supplied more than 120 sorties from units in Vietnam and Thailand. Units from Pleiku AB (A-1Es), Da Nang AB (F-4s), Cam Ranh Bay AB F-4s), Phu Cat AB (F-100s), and Takhli AB, Thailand (F-105s), helped hold back the communist attack until the evacuation was complete. There was also KC-135 tanker support from Thailand, and RF-101 and RF-4 reconnaissance sorties were flown over Kham Duc during the day to give the leadership in Saigon pictorial information to add to their knowledge of the tactical situation. By the time the fog lifted, around 0900, there were abundant fighters overhead to support the camp, although those on the ground could not see all of the aircraft waiting in orbit for their turn to drop ordnance on the enemy. In fact, there were more fighters in the air over Kham Duc than could be employed simultaneously or even profitably in the narrow confines of the Kham Duc bowl.[1]

ABCCC COORDINATION

The problem was not in gathering the air support, because this was nearly always forthcoming in Vietnam, but rather in controlling these assets. This was the responsibility of the ABCC and the FACs. Normally the ABCCC controlled fighters and bombers outside South Vietnam, but the use of the

ABCCC in South Vietnam was not unprecedented—it had been used at at Khe Sanh.[2] When the C-130 ABCCC was sent to Kham Duc on 12 May, however, it was not scheduled for that mission or that location; in fact it had been diverted to the Kham Duc area in mid-flight. The aircraft, with Col Claude Turner as senior controller and Capt Robert Gatewood as duty controller, had taken off at 0430 on 12 May and was diverted after having been airborne for two hours.[3] The only map of the Kham Duc area on board the aircraft was the C-130 navigator's JN chart, one with a scale of 1:2,000,000, which was unsuitable for close-tolerance fighter operations. Gatewood, who was more experienced at the mission than Turner (it was the colonel's first such mission on the ABCCC, having recently arrived in Vietnam), had to survey the area visually and draw freehand maps of the bowl and ridge line. While Gatewood was visually surveying the region, Turner was busy on the radios diverting aircraft from all over southeast Asia to the pressing needs of Kham Duc.[4]

Seventh Air Force, the designated single manager for air in Vietnam, helped Turner divert missions and formally directed the ABCCC, call sign Hillsboro, to take over on-scene command and control of the mission at 0900. From that moment on, until after the last people had been lifted off the littered and pockmarked runway, Hillsboro stayed overhead Kham Duc directing the fighter mission. Hillsboro controlled the tankers, assigned the fighters' parking orbits (in which they stayed awaiting their turn to deliver ordnance), and handed off the fighters to the FACs, who worked them in the terminal attack phases of their mission. ABCCC C-130s could remain in the air 16 hours, and Hillsboro almost reached its limit on 12 May. Although the coordination was incomplete (it had never been practiced and never really tried before) and Hillsboro had no contact with the Army and Marine helicopters and little with the Army ground commander, the ABCCC controllers performed a necessary coordination role and saw to it that the building plethora of tactical fighters was gainfully used. Had it not been for Hillsboro, the FACs, working in the tight constraints of the terrain above Kham Duc, would have been overwhelmed.[5]

THE TACTICAL SITUATION

While the ABCCC was establishing itself overhead, an Air Liaison Officer (ALO) from Chu Lai on the ground at Kham Duc was reporting into his personal tape recorder his view of the situation. He recorded the crash of the CH-47, the loss of the A-1E, and the damaging of the first C-130. The tone of his voice and his choice of adjectives demonstrate the seriousness of the situation. They show also that he did not know at 0800 (more than seven hours after the A Team was informed) that an evacuation had been ordered. After speaking of the three aircraft disasters, he remarked that "Charlie [the common nickname for communist forces] is on all sides," and that there had been no decision made yet whether to hold Kham Duc or get out: "We're in the midst of trying to decide whether to get out and let them have it or put up a big fight." All through the day there were indications of a command-and-control breakdown. The first CH-47 into Kham Duc was an evacuation

USAF ABCCC aircraft similar to Hillsboro.

Robert Gatewood, duty controller onboard Hillsboro on 12 May. Gatewood was an F-100 fighter pilot on loan to the ABCCC. He told the author that he was undecided about accepting a newly offered regular commission in the USAF until Kham Duc. He said, after observing the activities of the fighter crews, FACs and airlifters, that he made up his mind to join permanently that brotherhood.
Gatewood has recently been promoted to lieutenant colonel.

Interior of ABCCC, forward in the C-130.

Interior of ABCCC, the battle staff, to the rear of the C-130.

aircraft, but the first C-130 was carrying supplies and was, therefore, not sent into the camp to evacuate it.

The ALO remarked that airstrikes had been going on since 0300 but that the situation seemed to be worsening: "We've got more TAC air on the way, I hope to hell it gets here on time." When he came back to his tape recorder several hours later, he said, "Our position is becoming more untenable every minute," but by that time the ABCCC had several flights of fighters stacked up and was feeding the FACs as fast as they could absorb the fighters. Most of this was, of course, invisible to those on the ground. As the ALO spoke into his recorder, it picked up the sounds of artillery and mortar shells impacting and of outgoing rounds of fire as well as the sounds of jet aircraft and their bombs and cannon as the fighters struck back at the enemy. These sounds seem to punctuate the remarks of the ALO, and the longer the tape is played the greater the pressure seems to have been: "We've got beaucoup VC advancing on this field." Because the communists had used a tear gas attack on Ngoc Tavak, gas masks were handed out to the ALO and others on the ground at Kham Duc. The ALO, who could not see the building air support, recorded that he made an urgent request to I DASC for more tactical air support and that if this did not arrive soon "it's going to look pretty grim." He saw the enemy setting up a gun on the hill opposite the strip, and he knew that if the fighters could not destroy it, the Army and Air Force could not safely put helicopters or airplanes on the landing strip. Late in the morning he learned that the field was to be evacuated and that there were C130s programmed to evacuate the people and that everything of value was to be destroyed. He observed: "We've got a small Khe Sanh going on here: I hope we finish it before night comes."[6]

Some measure of the size of the enemy concentration about Kham Duc can be gleaned from an on-scene report of B-52s bombing the enemy position around Kham Duc after the last defenders and their dependents were airlifted out. On 13 May, 10 B-52 missions were devoted to Kham Duc, and 60 airplanes dropped 6,000 bombs within 500 yards of the runway. (There were also more missions on 14 May.) On just one of the missions on 13 May an observer recorded 78 secondary explosions during the strike, and some of these were ten times the magnitude of the bomb burst, while most of them were three times the magnitude. In all there were 130 secondary explosions recorded on 13 May, signifying an extraordinary concentration of enemy ordnance.[7]

Those on the ground, however, did not have to wait for the B-52 evidence to know that they were surrounded by a huge force, and early on 12 May they called I DASC for help. I DASC Log, which opened at 0510, indicated that an AC-47 Spooky gunship had arrived on station earlier to provide fire and flare support to the camp and that shortly thereafter, still several hours before sunrise, Helix 02, an Air Force 02 aircraft FAC, worked three sets of fighters in the area. I DASC kept 7th Air Force Tactical Air Control Center (TACC) apprised of the situation as the battle progressed. The log remarked that there "will be 20 C-130s going into there at 0900, so it should be interesting today."[8] Because there is no hint in the log that the C-130s were for other than emergency resupply, one suspects that at 0510 I DASC at Da Nang was unaware of the decision made well before midnight to evacuate the camp. This supposition is confirmed by material in the next chapter, which shows that the initial C-130 missions were not scheduled for evacuation.

By the time the first FAC arrived at 0515, General Momyer had been directed by MACV to evacuate Kham Duc.[9] At 0820 all units in 7th Air Force were alerted for a maximum effort at Kham Duc. Ten minutes later General Momyer initiated a "Grand Slam," code words used generally for maximum-effort assaults north of the demilitarized zone (DMZ), calling for an all-forces heavy firepower assault. Use of this term signified the extreme importance of the missions to Kham Duc. Momyer was notified that there were 110 fighter sorties available to him from outside Vietnam, and 121 sorties within Vietnam above and beyond the missions already programmed for that day. If needs became greater, another 85 sorties could be squeezed from out-of-country resources or diverted from missions of lesser importance.[10]

Even before Momyer had called for a Grand Slam, I DASC had been putting fighter support into Kham Duc. Between 0412 and 0900, when Hillsboro took over, I DASC had ordered 10 Marine A-4D fighter sorties and 18 Air Force aircraft (eight B-52s and 10 fighters) to Kham Duc. Most of these fighters were able to make eight ordnance delivery passes per sortie.

L-R: Gen W. C. Westmoreland, Gen J. P. McConnell, H. C. Lodge, Gen W. W. Momyer. Westmoreland was COMUSMACV, McConnell was Air Force Chief of Staff, Lodge was Ambassador to Viet Nam, and Momyer was 7AF Commander and the single manager for airpower in Viet Nam by the time of the Kham Duc evacuation. Photo was taken in February 1967.

Also during much of that period an AC-47 was on station providing suppressing fire with its 7.62 mm machine guns. It fired on the outposts in the hills, after they had been abandoned, to prevent their use by the communists, and fired directly into the two ravines which led from a stream that ran parallel to the runway and cut right up to the camp perimeter. An estimated three enemy companies were using these ravines, shielded by the forest, to advance on the camp. By the time the first FAC arrived at 0515, it was already obvious that more than Spooky's machine guns were needed to save the people in the camp.[11]

THE FAC MISSION

The FACs were the airmen responsible for directing the fighter attacks on targets. The first FAC at Kham Duc on 12 May was Capt Herbert J. Spier, an Air Force 0-2 pilot working with the Americal Division at Chu Lai AB. He arrived well before daybreak and more than three hours before the ABCCC. Spier's first sets of fighters were worked with a C-47 flare ship providing light for the fighter aircraft crews. This flare ship had replaced the AC-47 gunship. Spier put in three F-4s on multiple passes on targets before it became light enough to see them without the aid of flares. But when the sun came up, so did the morning fog, and nearly the entire area was blanketed by fog before the fourth set of fighters arrived. Because Spier had managed (with the help of the flareship) to become familiar with the terrain and the enemy positions before the sun and fog came up, he was able to direct the

USAF 0-2 aircraft similar to those used by all the FACs who controlled airplanes over Kham Duc on 12 May.

fighters even though most of the ground was obscured. He assigned altitudes and let the fighters line up on his aircraft, and told the crews when to drop their ordnance. He was able to put the bombs within six to seven hundred meters of the camp perimeter this way. The ALO on the ground could not see the FAC nor the fighters, but he could see and hear the bombs impacting, and he was able to help Spier move the bombs closer to the camp perimeter and onto better targets. Spier stayed on station for two and one-half hours before being relieved and in that time worked 10 fighters. Although he was replaced after 0730, he came back to Kham Duc in the afternoon and was on station for the last of the evacuation.[12] He remarked into a tape recorder that Kham Duc "was the most hectic situation I have been involved in," and "I hope I don't have to be involved in a similar situation for the rest of my tour here."[13]

Spier came from Chu Lai AB, and he and most of the FACs there were familiar with the problem at Kham Duc, because the chief ALO for I Corp, Lt Col Reese B. Black from Chu Lai, had flown an 0-1 aircraft into the camp on 11 May to survey the deteriorating situation. Black arranged for a ground-based ALO to stay with the Americal Division battalion and Special Forces A Team to assure the defenders that tactical air would be available. He was replaced at the camp by Capt Willard C. Johnson, and Black returned to Chu Lai to brief the pilots. He also spent a good part of 12 May above Kham Duc as a FAC directing fighters.[14]

Because of Black's knowledge of the situation and Johnson's urgent requests to I DASC for help, when Spier departed he was replaced by teams of FACs, sometimes as many as five, to provide direction to the fighters. It soon became apparent that four or five FACs were too many, and soon after the fog cleared and Hillsboro began operating, the FACs devised a system by which only three FACs were simultaneously employed. Two FACs flew at the same altitude, parallel to one another over opposite sides of the Kham Duc runway. Each controlled fighters striking targets on his side of the runway. The third FAC flew below the ABCCC and at an altitude above the two FACs working opposite sides of the runway. He took aircraft from Hillsboro and fed them to the FAC that needed the ordnance load being carried by the fighter or to the FAC with the more urgent need. When the transports returned to Kham Duc in the late afternoon, the FACs had the fighters suppress ground fire on the routes used by the aircraft, and Hillsboro and the FACs tried to sequence the transports and fighters together so that the fighters could serve as a sort of escort. Sometimes fighters made their protective passes no more than 100 feet off the C-130 wing tips. The fighters were also directed by the FACs to other areas around Kham Duc when the targets were more important than the enemy closest to the field and camp.[15]

Hillsboro, who usually had four aircraft flights stacked and waiting to go in, also kept track of the ordnance the fighters were carrying and passed this information to the high-altitude FAC, who then asked the two FACs working the runway what they needed in the way of ordnance. In other

USAF 0-1 aircraft similar to the one used by Reese Black to fly into Kham Duc on 11 May. The 0-1 was also a FAC aircraft.

Reese Black receiving the Silver Star for his actions at Kham Duc. BGen E. L. Little is presenting the medal.

0-2 aircraft similar to the ones flown over Kham Duc on 12 May. The pilot is James Gibler who was a FAC at Kham Duc.

words, there was such an abundance of fighters by late morning that the FACs could choose the fighter they wanted, based on whether it carried napalm, cluster-bomb units, 500- or 750-pound bombs, or high-drag bombs for low-altitude delivery. Each of these weapons was more suitable for one type target than for another. The fighters came in with varied ordnance because of the variety of targets at Kham Duc. So called "soft ordnance" like CBUs and napalm was very effective against enemy troops in the open but tended to skip along the top of the jungle canopy or singe it instead of penetrating to the jungle floor when the enemy had to be attacked there. The more popular ordnance when the enemy was partly hidden was 500–pound and especially 750–pound bombs with instantaneous fuses. These gave better coverage and penetrated the jungle canopy without digging a large hole upon detonation. When the enemy was sighted in a clearing near the runway, which was the camp's asphalt lifeline, the FACs could reject airplanes carrying hard ordnance, and call on an aircraft with CBU or napalm, which was more effective against troops in the open. The FACs would either send the fighters they had rejected back into orbit to await a more propitious moment, up to a waiting KC-135 tanker (on station since early morning) to take on fuel in order to remain longer in the area and later rejoin the fighter stack in parking orbit, or even back home, if there was a surfeit of a particular type of ordnance in the stack and Hillsboro was saturated.[16] Tactical airpower proved responsive to the Army's needs at Kham Duc. Lt Col Richard P. Schuman, the senior ALO for the Americal Division, was one of the early FACs on station, and he was able to work pairs of fighters as quickly as every 45 seconds. After a morning mission which lasted about four hours he returned to Kham Duc and was on scene at the final stages of the evacuation in the afternoon.[17]

FAC SMOTHERMAN'S ORDEAL

Another FAC who worked morning missions was Capt Philip R. Smotherman, who saw Kham Duc from all the vantage points—more, in fact, than he desired. He was knowledgeable about the emergency because he had been working the radios in the Americal Division tactical operations center (TOC) as the offensive against the camp was brewing, and he knew of the desperation of the defenders. He took off from Chu Lai in mid-morning and arrived over Kham Duc at approximately 1030, after about a half-hour flight. Initially he was the high-altitude FAC, and after that role he controlled aircraft on one side of the runway. He put his first set of fighters onto a known .50-caliber gun position and silenced the guns with some "very quick and accurate work" from a pair of F-100s. He then controlled a pair of Marine A-4Ds with rockets. While directing the fighters his 0-2 was struck by enemy fire, and his right wing tip was shot off. Smotherman lost control of the aircraft ailerons, and the elevator soon bound up. He had only rudder and engines for control. At first he thought he might be forced to bail out or crash land outside the camp perimeter, but then believed he could land on the airstrip if his luck held out. After having started for the field and begun his descent, he was almost run over by a departing C-123. Dodging the C-123 almost cost him his chance for crash landing on the airstrip. Smotherman

Philip Smotherman beside his 0-2 aircraft, similar to the one he crash-landed at Kham Duc on 12 May.

made a controlled crash and subsequently was able to move the 0-2 off the runway so that it would not block further evacuations. He cut off the switches and jumped out of the airplane, now an enemy artillery target. A moment later he was picked up by a Special Forces sergeant, who rushed him into the A Team command bunker as mortars struck around his aircraft. Smotherman had joined those on the ground shortly after 1110.[18]

There were no radios in the Special Forces bunker with which Smotherman could call I DASC to let them know of his situation, so he went to the tactical air control party (TACP) bunker to radio I DASC. Soon thereafter, Smotherman was told by I DASC that he had been ordered by General Momyer to remain on the ground at Kham Duc as the ALO, because at that point he was the only Air Force officer on the scene. Smotherman spent the next five hours doing what he could to translate the ground personnel's needs to the ABCCC and the FACs. He stayed in contact with I DASC at Da Nang (which gave him some information on incoming transports) and passed information to the outside world concerning the numbers of people left on the ground for pickup. He also tried to set up the defenders for evacuation. Smotherman was able to work in several instances as a ground FAC, directing the fighters on strikes as close as 30 meters from his bunker. On one such strike, necessary because of the proximity of the enemy, Smotherman got dust in his hair from the concussion and felt the heat of the napalm. During the afternoon he was slightly wounded by enemy mortar fragments, but the wounds did not hinder him. He left Kham Duc on the last passenger-carrying C-130, along with the remainder of the Special Forces leaders and some CIDG troops.[19] In the air and on the ground, Smotherman had performed a very important mission.

When Smotherman was in the air and while he was on the ground, he was in contact with the American Division's TACP. He and the other FAC pilots passed information about the situation to the TACP at Chu Lai about the types of loads needed and the status of the defenders and Vietnamese dependents. At times General Koster's headquarters lost contact with Colonel Nelson, and for a while Koster was worried that the camp had actually been overrun. Through Smotherman and the other FACs, however, Koster learned that the tactical fighters had been holding off the enemy while the helicopters and Air Force transports were bringing out his people.[20]

THE FIGHTER MISSION

For all of Smotherman's work and the coordination and control efforts of the ABCCC and other FACs, without the fighters all would have been lost. The fighter aircraft carried heavy loads—up to 5,000 pounds of bombs in the F-4s—and their 20 mm cannon, rockets, and bombs provided the narrow margin of whatever victory could be claimed.[21]

One of the first targets for the fighters was the same gully that the AC-47 had cleaned out in the early morning. Here again in the ravines and low ground to the east and south of the runway the enemy formed successive attacks which would have brought them to the midpoint of the runway if they had succeeded. With North Vietnamese troops already on the outer

USAF AC-47 gunships.

wire perimeter of the fence the fighters dropped napalm and CBUs on them to drive them back. Attacks continued in this quarter all day, despite the terrific losses the communists took from the air strikes.[22] As the day went on the fighter pilots noted that they were bombing closer and closer to the camp perimeter because the enemy persistently pressed forward. Often the fighter crews could see the enemy on the fence trying to break into the compound.[23]

Other frequently struck targets were the abandoned outposts. Apparently some of the men who had been in these positions on the high ground around the camp had been unable to destroy their weapons before abandoning the posts. Some of the North Vietnamese were able to turn the outposts' .50 caliber machine guns on the camp as well as on the aircraft defending it and trying to land to evacuate it.[24]

USAF A-1E fighter aircraft.

USAF A-1E fighter aircraft.

Marine A-4 fighter aircraft.

Vietnamese Air Force F-5 fighter aircraft.

Late in the day the enemy had come so close to the camp's dwindling defenders that one of the Special Forces officers inside the A Team bunker was able to mark an enemy position with a smoke grenade. As soon as it was so highlighted, an A-1E dropped napalm on the enemy concentration, which was so close that the Army officer was rocked by the concussion and felt the heat of the napalm.[25] Although the FACs avoided using fighters with hard ordnance within 100 meters of friendly troops, they had no compunction against using those with napalm in such proximity, because they were confident of the accuracy of the fighter crews, who had been improving as the day went on. At times napalm was dropped on the friendly side of the perimeter fence to drive the enemy off it. Throughout the evacuation the enemy was never able to penetrate the perimeter.[26]

During the attack, the fighters pressed in so close to the friendly troops that Colonel Nelson had to ask them to back off because of his concern for his men—none of whom, however, was wounded by friendly ordnance.[27] As the day wore on, furthermore, strikes had to be put in even more rapidly as the number of defenders dwindled. At the end of the day, all those who might have been at the perimeter keeping the enemy at bay were busy making their way to the runway to be airlifted out. At the end, most of the ordnance was delivered within 150 to 200 meters of the last defenders and some of it within 25 meters,[28] less than the distance from homeplate to first base. After the evacuation was complete, these same fighters, now without concern for friendly troops, destroyed the several aircraft that had been disabled and abandoned at Kahm Duc, as well as the Army and Air Force equipment left behind.[29]

USAF F-100 fighter aircraft dropping general purpose bomb.

Walter Hersman, an F-100 pilot who supported the evacuation of Kham Duc on 12 May. Photo taken on Hersman's next assignment as an F-104 pilot.

USAF F-4 fighter aircraft.

Of all the fighter activities on 12 May, most important were those that provided assistance to the helicopters and transports evacuating the 1,400 people. In the last hour of the evacuation, seven C-130s and two C-123s landed at Kham Duc, an impossible feat without the fighters.

USAF F-105 fighter aircraft.

CHAPTER **IV**

Tactical Airlift At Kham Duc

INTRODUCTION

Although the decision to evacuate Kham Duc was made on 11 May, and the Special Forces A Team was so advised just after midnight, the 834th Air Division, which controlled all Air Force airlift in Vietnam, was not told to extract people from the camp until about 0800 on 12 May. Two possible reasons for this delay come to mind: either the Army or Marines, or both, intended to attempt the extraction of all the people with helicopters while the camp was under severe pressure, or there was a breakdown in command and control. At 0820 General Momyer told the 834th to make a maximum effort to extract the people, and at that moment there must have been some thought of salvaging the equipment, because the 834th was told that there were 50 tons of it at Kham Duc. But by 1030 the ground fire had become so intense that a C-130 made an airdrop of ammunition into the camp because it was not safe to land and off-load supplies. At about the same time, the 7th Air Force radioed that it was "completely unfeasible" to carry out any evacuation by C-130s, reversed its decision of several hours earlier, and cancelled the C-130 evacuation. The 834th ALCC began to prepare a massive airdrop of ammunition into Kham Duc. Three hours later, however, MACV ordered the 834th to resume the extraction, because time was running out, and there was no other way to bring out the remaining people.[1]

THE DECISION TO EVACUATE WITH C-130S

The rapidly changing airlift mission caused some confusion among aircrews and field detachments of the 834th. By early morning the aircrews and aircraft under the control of the 834th were prepared for an emergency resupply mission. As the deteriorating position became better known by daybreak, the airlift control element (ALCE) at Da Nang (a detachment of the 834th Air Division), lined up several C-123s and C-130s fully loaded with ammunition and rigged for air drop into the beleagured camp.[2] These aircraft stayed on alert with their rigged loads throughout the entire day in case of need.[3] At the time of the cancellation of the C-130 missions in the

Burl W. McLaughlin, Commander of the 834th Air Division.

morning (approximately 1030) there were three C-130s and one C-123 over
Kham Duc in a holding pattern waiting for an opportunity to land.[4]

When the MACV combat operations center (COC) directed the 834th
ALCC to resume extractions by C-130s and C-123s at 1315,[5] the ALCEs
at the various airlift bases (Tan Son Nhut, Cam Ranh Bay, Phan Rang, and
Da Nang) had to reconfigure aircraft. Some airplanes were airborne with
loads of supplies on them, and some were being rigged for airdrop; now
everything had to be derigged and downloaded to prepare the airplanes for
an evacuation.[6] On the morning of 12 May, some aircrews were already
taxiing out with loads for Kham Duc when they were told to hold their
positions and await further instructions. Soon the crews were told to shut
down their engines and prepare to rig for airdrop. This was a time-
consuming operation. After loads rigged for paradropping were brought
out to the aircraft and the loadmasters had prepared the C-130s for drops,
the crews were told to empty their airplanes and to fly to Kham Duc to take
out as many soldiers and Vietnamese dependents as they could carry. One

experienced aircraft commander remarked that the "ship was without a rudder," and "confusion reigned supreme."[7]

Meanwhile at Kham Duc, the Special Forces leaders, who had been expecting an evacuation since midnight, were arranging an order of evacuation from the camp. Some confusion arose over the sequence of departures. The Special Forces were eager to remain at the camp until the end so that they could maintain discipline with the irregular troops. The A Team wanted the dependents out first and the irregulars to leave with the engineers and Americal Division personnel. Apparently they were informed that General Koster and General Cushman wanted the CIDG and other indigenous forces to be the last out, and so directed the movement of all Americans to the airstrip for earliest evacuation. Captain Henderson refused to follow these orders and tried, as best he could, to impose his order on the evacuation. He feared that there would have been "total panic" among the Vietnamese if they realized that they were going to be left for last, and he doubted that the Vietnamese would see anything other than abandonment in such a move. Henderson believed that the Special Forces were the only "true link" between the Americans and the Vietnamese, and he feared a "catastrophe" if the last people on the ground were to be Vietnamese.[8] Given the poor performance of some of the irregulars at Ngoc Tavak and at Kham Duc during the ground battle, the Special Forces, by disregarding these orders from a higher headquarters, probably saved some lives.

THE FIRST C-130 INTO KHAM DUC ON 12 MAY

Symbolic of the panic of the Vietnamese was their rush to board the first C-130 that got into the camp in the early morning. This airplane had landed after the CH-47 wreckage had been cleared from the runway, but the C-130 had taken so many hits that it was not able to take off with a load of evacuees and the cargo they had prevented the loadmaster from offloading. The aircraft and crew, unaware that they were on an evacuating mission, were on temporary duty to Cam Ranh Bay from Naha Air Base, Okinawa. They landed at Kham Duc in a hail of mortar shells, on a runway littered with spent cartridges and debris, with a flat tire and many holes in the main fuel tanks in the wing. The next problem the crew had to cope with was the hysterical hundred or so Vietnamese civilians and irregular troops who rushed the aircraft from the ditches alongside the runway. The people could not be budged from the cargo compartment so that the aircraft could be offloaded. The longer the airplane was on the ground the more it was exposed to mortar and rocket fire (C-130s always invited artillery attacks). The aircraft commander, Lt Col Daryl D. Cole, decided to launch with the Vietnamese onboard even though part of the load was still on the airplane. With fuel pouring out of the wing tanks and with a flat tire, Cole tried to get up enough speed to get his C-130 into the air. The blown tire and the load of civilians and the cargo they had prevented the loadmaster from offloading were too much for the airplane, however, and Cole aborted the take off, taxied off the runway, and discharged the passengers. The crew decided to cut off the blown tire to stop it from flapping and slowing down the C-130 on

USAF C-130 taking off from Kham Duc.

take off roll. While cutting at it with a bayonet, mortars shells impacted all around them. They succeeded in cutting off the rubber, but could not cut through the steel beading with the bayonet. They next tried to cut the beading with a blow torch but without much effect. All the time the mortars struck nearer, and a 105 mm howitzer no more than 10 yards from their position received a direct hit. Cole then realized that it would be only a few minutes before the enemy got the range. He decided to try again to get enough speed to fly. With three engines running the aircraft taxied onto the runway; starting the number one engine was delayed because of fear that a fire would be caused by the fuel pouring out that side of the wing. Taxiing was proving to be difficult because a disabled 3/4-ton truck partly blocked the right side of the ramp. The aircraft had to be taxied over cargo and equipment with care so that none of the propellers struck any objects. The number 1 engine was started on the runway, and as Cole aligned the C-130 with the ramp, two mortar shells struck so close to the airplane that two windows on the right side of the cockpit were shattered by the concussion. Cole then had to fight the problem of the blown tire and the fuel imbalance caused by the punctured fuel tanks. The C-130 had lost 4,000 pounds of fuel from the right side of the airplane. Cole, perhaps with skills born of desperation, was able to get the C-130 airborne and safely back to Cam Ranh Bay. After landing, the maintenance crew counted more than 85 bullet and shrapnel holes in Cole's aircraft.[9]

On board Cole's airplane were four passengers: the combat control team (CCT) and the ALO. The commander of the CCT had ordered the two enlisted men serving at Kham Duc with him to board this airplane. He had heard that there would be no further C-130 evacuations, and he believed that his mission was over. The two enlisted members of the CCT objected because they thought they would still have a mission even without a resupply or evacuation. They knew they would be needed to control the airdrops that would surely follow if the fixed-wing evacuation were terminated. These two men, Technical Sergeant (TSgt) Morton Freedman and Staff Sergeant (SSgt) James Lundie, were unable to convince their mission commander, Maj John Gallagher (who was not a combat controller but, rather, a C-130 pilot), and were forced to board Cole's C-130. Also onboard was the ground ALO, Capt Willard Johnson.[10]

Soon after Cole departed with his stricken C-130 and small load, one of the overhead C-123s, piloted by Maj Ray D. Shelton, landed and took out 65 people: 44 Army engineers and 21 civilian Vietnamese. Shelton reported that there was intense ground fire from every quadrant, and mortar shells hit all around him after landing.[11] He was on the ground for no more than three minutes.[12] At this time—about 1110—some 145 people had been evacuated from Kham Duc by helicopter, Cole's C-130, and Shelton's C-123.[13] The toll in aircraft losses and battle damage was already high.

Gen J. D. Ryan, USAF Chief of Staff, presenting Daryl Cole the 1968 McKay Trophy for the Air Force's "most meritorious flight of the year." Cole received the Silver Star for saving his C-130 at Kham Duc.

USAF C-123 transport aircraft similar to Shelton's airplane.

THE SECOND C-130 INTO KHAM DUC

The price got higher in the afternoon. It was three hours between Shelton's departure and the arrival of the next fixed-wing aircraft, a C-130 from Tan Son Nhut AB. C-130s stationed there were in Vietnam on temporary duty from Mactan AB, in the southern Philippines, or Clark AB, in Luzon. This airplane was piloted by Maj Bernard L. Bucher of Mactan. His airplane was struck by ground fire many times on its final approach into the airstrip from the southwest. After taking on a full load (at least 150 and maybe as many as 200 or more Vietnamese women and children), Bucher took off to the northeast. This turned out to be an unfortunate choice, but was probably based on the ground fire Bucher had received while landing from the southwest. Soon after takeoff, Bucher's airplane was riddled by groundfire and crashed in a huge ball of orange flame less than a mile from the end of the runway. No one survived the crash.[14]

The most intense ground fire Bucher's airplane received came from a knoll to the north of the runway. Captain Spier, the first FAC on duty that morning and now back on duty again, saw two .50 caliber machine guns rake Bucher's C-130. Spier called immediately for a fighter strike and within 30 seconds he had a fighter drop CBUs onto the machine gun position, destroying it. Spier continued to watch the ridge and nest until the end of the evacuation, but he saw no further muzzle flashes.[15]

"FOR GOD'S SAKE STAY OUT OF KHAM DUC.
IT BELONGS TO CHARLIE"

Bucher was shot down around 1530, which meant that there had not been successful C-130 evacuation mission from Kham Duc. The weather was beginning to close in as night was approaching, but there were more than 600 people still on the ground. The next C-130 into the camp also was hit many times, but it fared better. Lt Col William Boyd, Jr., saw Bucher's airplane crash and explode in a ravine north of the runway. He noted later that he had never in his career seen so many tracer bullets fired at an object. Boyd had known before he took off for Kham Duc that it was going to be a dangerous mission. Before being diverted to the camp from an airlift mission into Chu Lai, he talked to the A-1E pilot who had been shot down and rescued in the early morning. He was told: "For God's sake stay out of Kham Duc. It belongs to Charlie." After watching Bucher's crash, Boyd pulled back on his throttles and began a steep, sideslipping descent into the field. He did this to minimize the time in descent in order to leave his aircraft exposed for the least amount of time. Boyd and his crew could actually see the enemy taking aim and firing their AK-47s at them from the area around the perimeter fence, and he took numerous hits as he dived for the field. Just before he was about to touch down, a shell exploded 100 feet in front of his airplane, and Boyd was forced to push the throttles forward. He pulled up and went around for a second approach. C-130 crews abhorred having to make multiple passes or "go arounds" because the big airplane became an obvious target with a predictable flight path. Boyd and his crew decided to make the

The remains of Bucher's C-130.

second approach because they could see the people on the ground and knew how desperate they were. As Boyd landed, people poured out of the ditches beside the runway and rushed his airplane. Since Bucher had not succeeded with a northeast takeoff, Boyd decided to depart to the southwest. He turned his aircraft around and took off, suffering numerous hits on takeoff roll and during climb out. When he landed at Cam Ranh Bay the ground crew counted holes in the sides of the fuselage, the left wing, the leading edge of both wings and generally all over the airplane. One of the men rescued took a can of spray paint and wrote "Lucky Duc" on the side of Boyd's C-130[16]. Boyd's crew rescued more than 100 people, but the next C-130 crew was not so fortunate.

THE FOURTH C-130 INTO KHAM DUC

This aircraft was under the command of Lt Col John Delmore, out of Cam Ranh Bay on temporary duty from Naha AB in Okinawa. Delmore was about to land when Boyd was taking off, so he had to make a go around. Delmore and his crew had also witnessed Bucher's crash and could not have relished the second pass. Near the end of his next approach, at about 300 to 400 feet altitude, the airplane began to take hits. The crew likened the sounds of the rounds hitting the skin of the airplane to that of sledgehammer blows. While still several hundred yards from touchdown, smoke began to curl up through the floorboards of the cockpit between the pilot's legs. Seconds later the sides of the cockpit were opened by bullets that made six inch holes in the aluminum skin. The engineer, TSgt John McCall, saw bullets come up

William Boyd presented with the Air Force Cross for his action at Kham Duc on 12 May. Lt Gen F. C. Gideon is presenting the award.

through the floor and tear holes in the roof of the cockpit. The enemy, obviously aiming for the flight crew, was able to force the airplane over on its side just before touchdown, but the pilot and copilot fought to right the airplane; all four engines were shut down because they were now running out of control. Seconds before impact McCall jettisoned the crew-entrance door so that the crew could use that exit for escape. When the C-130 struck the runway, its wheels were down, but the hydraulic system had failed completely, and there were no brakes and little directional control. Delmore crashed into the CH-47 that had been destroyed early in the morning and turned his C-130 off the runway as not to block it. He ran the airplane into a dirt mound to stop its progress. With the airplane stopped nearly entirely off the runway, all five of the crew got out as quickly as they could. Being armed only with .38 caliber pistols, they thought themselves nearly naked because of the heavy enemy ground fire. Fortunately they were not on the ground for more than 20 minutes when a Marine CH-46 took them out of the Kham Duc cauldron to safety.[17]

THE END OF THE AIRLIFT EVACUATION

Lt Col Franklin Montgomery had watched Bucher's airplane go down and Delmore's C-130 crash and burn on the runway, yet despite these two disasters, he descended right over the field and landed in a hail of tracer fire. Montgomery taxied his aircraft quickly by the crashed CH-47 and the destroyed C-130 and took on a full load of people as fast as they could run onto the airplane. His crew counted more than 50 mortar shells or rockets impacting in the area of the C-130 in the few minutes it was on the ground. Soon more than 150 Vietnamese civilians, a handful of CIDG forces, and a few Army troops were onboard. The Vietnamese civilians and some of the irregulars were so panic stricken and hysterical that they ran underneath the spinning propellers to board the airplane. The loadmaster, trying to maintain order, was knocked down and trampled by the Vietnamese and knocked down another time by the concussion of a nearby mortar shell. By this time, after 1600, the field was in such straits that no one in the air or on the ground could tell Montgomery whom he was picking up, where they were, or what the condition of the runway was. Montgomery's C-130 suffered no hits, remarkable when one considers the battle damage done to the previous two C-130s.[18] As Montgomery lifted off, another C-130 landed and took on 130 people. When this airplane got airborne another landed, taking off 90. Neither of these took any battle damage.[19] At the last, things seemed to improve.

There were now only a few people remaining on the ground at Kham Duc. Among them were Captain Smotherman and Captain Henderson, some Special Forces troops, and CIDG officers and men—about one C-130 load.

Maj James L. Wallace flew his C-130 into Kham Duc to extract them. As Wallace prepared to land, General Momyer was directing the ALCC to stop using C-130s for the evacuation because of the high losses. But before he could get his orders to the field the last of the defenders and civilians had been picked up by Wallace and his crew. While they were on the ground, the camp's ammunition dumps began to explode, and the crew observed hysteria among the Vietnamese soldiers because they had lost families on Bucher's C-130. Although Wallace's airplane was fired upon, it also took no hits. Captain Smotherman reported that the tension of everybody inside the plane began to evaporate as it gained altitude, and by the time the airplane had climbed fully out of the bowl and leveled off on its way to the coast the reduction of tension was noticeable. Smotherman believed that "nothing could top this experience," and he hoped that in the rest of his tour nothing would. He recorded that he had been confident that he would escape from Kham Duc because "there were so many good guys on our side."[20]

Good guys indeed. There had been eight C-130s into Kham Duc to that point on 12 May. Six of these were able to get some passengers back to safety, and two were destroyed. Of the six successful C-130s, one was able to take out only four people, and the remaining five took out more than 600. Also one C-123 took out 65 people in the late morning. The rest of the people at Kham Duc on 12 May who survived the communist small arms and artillery fire either were rescued by helicopter or died on Bucher's airplane. The costs were high: seven aircraft lost, many helicopters damaged, and three C-130s with major battle damage.[21]

THE CCT REINSERTED

But the day was not over yet. As Wallace was racing down the runway to take off, another C-130, this one with three passengers on board, was about to land and reinsert the CCT. They had been ordered back by General McLaughlin, Commander of the 834th AD, who did so when he discovered, in the early afternoon, that they had left the job before it was complete. But when the CCT arrived back at Kham Duc the last passengers they were to assist were already airborne. This command and control breakdown was caused by confusion, noise over the radios, excitement, distances between the ABCCC and other overhead control elements and the ALCC at Saigon, and late reporting by those on the ground of the actual numbers of people remaining. The crew that inserted the CCT did not know that General McLaughlin himself was now overhead to direct the mission, and when they were in the landing pattern no one they could talk to was aware of the fact that Major Wallace had just lifted the last of the Kham Duc contingent off the runway. When the three-man CCT left their C-130 there was no one on the ground to protect them but themselves.[22]

Edward Carr, C-130 navigator on the aircraft that reinserted the CCT

Aerial view of Kham Duc runway seconds before the CCT landed on 12 May.
Bright flashes are fires and explosions.

Ammunition dump exploding at Kham Duc seconds after the CCT landed.

USAF Combat Controllers and their equipment at Kham Duc. Photo taken after Kham Duc was reoccupied by US forces in 1970.

CHAPTER V

The Last Three Men at Kham Duc

INTRODUCTION

These three men had seen a great deal of action since they had landed at Kham Duc on 10 May on what was supposed to be a routine mission to assist the C-130s in the airlanding of the Americal Division battalion. From the time they landed until they left in the late morning of 12 May, they helped expedite 24 aircraft into Kham Duc. With their radios they advised aircrews of the best approaches into the camp and the safest ways out, and they helped the crews to offload the C-130s rapidly to shorten their ground time because the airlifters made excellent targets. Two of the men on the team were parachute-jump, professionally qualified combat controllers: Freedman and Lundie. The third man, Major Gallagher, was not a combat controller. He was, however, a qualified C-130 pilot (which, of course, Freedman and Lundie were not) and could be expected to give advice to aircrews from that standpoint. Gallagher was the mission commander because it was routine to place a commissioned officer above enlisted men such as Freedman and Lundie on missions similar to Kham Duc.[1]

The CCT had been under fire since it arrived on 10 May, and much of the equipment they needed to function had been damaged or destroyed in the three days they were on the ground. No sooner had they landed on 10 May when a mortar blew up their jeep trailer, which contained some radios, small arms and other needed material. Minutes later another round impacted near them, and the shrapnel wounded a nearby Army sergeant. Freedman pulled this man into a ditch beside the runway and gave him first aid. Seconds later another mortar round struck near the team, and the shrapnel from it further wounded the Army sergeant. Soon there were C-130s stacked up over the camp and Freedman and Lundie worked in the most difficult of situations to get them on and off the ground in rapid order with less than the usual array of combat-control equipment to assist them. Trying between sorties to rescue materiel from the jeep trailer, Lundie broke his hand. A Special Forces medic tried to talk him into being evacuated because of the severity of the break, but Lundie refused because he believed he was too important to the mission. In the afternoon of 10 May, Freedman and Lundie noted a three-mortar-shell barrage bracket their radio jeep. Freedman ordered it moved immediately, but before it had rolled more than 10 meters, another barrage struck the ground on which it had stood, the concussion knocking down the two sergeants. Eventually mortar shells destroyed their radio jeep. Each time mortar shells or rockets or other artillery pressed in on them, the two combat controllers took refuge in the ditch beside the runway.[2]

THE RETURN TO KHAM DUC

Having been reluctant to leave Kham Duc when ordered by their mission commander, neither Lundie nor Freedman was overly upset when the three-man team was told to return shortly after their arrival at Cam Ranh Bay on Cole's crippled C-130. The CCT was taken out to another C-130, this one under the command of Maj Jay Van Cleeff. The aircrew of this airplane had been diverted from another mission and had arrived at Cam Ranh Bay at 1240. They went immediatley to the ALCE and received an airdrop mission briefing for Kham Duc. They were told that it was "too dangerous to land at Kham Duc," and that after the briefing they were to proceed to Da Nang to pick up a container delivery system (CDS) load of emergency supplies to be paradropped into Kham Duc. They called the ALCE after engines start to tell the control element that they were taxiing to take off for Da Nang. Van Cleeff and crew were told that they were to await three passengers for Kham Duc. The crew was mystified: they had been told that they were to make a CDS airdrop into the camp because it was too dangerous to land, and now they were being told to airland some people. The CCT was brought out, and Gallagher tried to explain to Van Cleeff the futility of his mission because most of the CCT equipment had been destroyed and fixed wing extractions had been called off—what good would the CCT do there? On the way out to the runway Gallagher tried to explain this to the ALCE, but to no avail. On the way to Kham Duc he talked to the ALCC at Saigon, call sign Hilda, but was told to stop cluttering the airways. The crew was airborne at 1500 and landed at Kahm Duc about 1620. While in the landing pattern, they saw what was to be the last C-130 evacuation airplane take off from Kahm Duc, but they did not know that; in fact no one in the air over Kham Duc was to know that for a few minutes. After disembarking the CCT, Van Cleeff and crew waited on the ground for five minutes for them to return. There was no one on the ground to take out, and as they waited mortar shells marched closer and closer to their aircraft; when the aircrew began to see tracer and machine gun bullets striking the ground alongside the airplane, they decided to wait no more. Not knowing that General McLaughlin was overhead, and not knowing what their precise responsibilities were after the CCT was reinserted, they decided to save the airplane and took off. They flew away from Kham Duc empty because there was no one left on the ground but the CCT. After being airborne for a few seconds,the crew heard someone say over the radios that the camp was fully evacuated and could now be destroyed at will. This call was probably made by the C-130 that had taken off while Van Cleeff's airplane was on final approach. Van Cleeff hurriedly called: "Negative, negative," announcing to all that could hear (and apparently punctuating his remarks with profanity born of need for emphasis and out of frustration) that he had just inserted a three-man CCT into Kham Duc.[3]

Up to that moment there had been cacophony over the airwaves as fighters, FACs, ABCCC, and transports tried to work out their tactical problems. When Van Cleeff spoke his piece, an "unreal" silence came over the radios.[4] Gatewood, duty controller of the ABCCC, who had believed seconds earlier that his long mission was over, must have felt sick when he heard Van Cleeff, and he remembered that a "hush could be felt, literally, over the radio" as all agencies realized the implications of Van Cleeff's statement.[5]

THE CCT ON THE GROUND ALONE

Of course the CCT did not know how close they came to being killed by friendly aircraft. When they left the C-130, they ran to the Special Forces compound to gather people to evacuate, but they found no one alive there and the compound engulfed in flames. They crossed the runway and ran to the American Division battalion command post and then to the artillery compound, only to find those empty too. They became confused, then sickened, realizing that they were on the field alone and that the enemy was closing in on them.[6]

They ran back to the ditch they had spent so much time in earlier in the day, as well as on 10 and 11 May, and waited for a miracle. Freedman tried to talk to the aircraft overhead with his emergency UHF radio, only to find that it was disabled. Lundie and Freedman nearly gave up hope. They had only a few hundred rounds of M-16 ammunition with them and their .38 caliber revolvers. They could see the North Vietnamese setting up machine gun positions on either side of the runway—one of which was under the wing of Delmore's crashed C-130. Freedman and Lundie were determined not to surrender and decided to watch opposite ends of the runway for the enemy and to make the communists pay for taking them by killing as many of the enemy as they could. In the emotional heat of their dilemma, Freedman told Lundie to take his wallet because there was a lot of money in it and he did not want the North Vietnamese to get it; he told Lundie to make sure his wife did. To help themselves out, Freedman killed at least one, and probably both, of the men in the machine gun nest under the wing of Delmore's C-130 and disabled the gun. After a burst of M-16 fire one of the men keeled over, and the gun no longer fired at them. The machine gun on the opposite side of the runway, however, continually fired at them, and, worse, a group of men was approaching them from the extreme west end of the runway.[7]

Freedman and Lundie were convinced that no one in his "right mind" would land on the Kham Duc runway now with the enemy on it. To make matters worse, the ammunition dumps were blowing up. Worst of all, because Freedman had been unable to talk to the overhead aircraft by radio, no one could be sure that the CCT was still alive. Freedman said he "never felt so lonely in all my life."[8]

After sending several FACs to make relatively low passes over the field to locate the team—unsuccessfully as it turned out—Gatewood called on the next aircraft in the stack to land on the asphalt strip to see if the men might come out of hiding with an airplane on the ground—that is, if they were still alive. Without hesitation Lt Col Alfred J. Jeanotte, Jr., and crew throttled back, nosed their C-123 over, and dove for the runway. Bookie 750, Jeanotte's call sign, had been overhead for some time, and the crew knew the risks involved. But they also knew that there was only one hope of saving the three men: to land and pick them up. If Jeanotte failed, there were other aircraft that would try. Next in line was another C-123, and third in line was General McLaughlin. Gatewood got fighter aircraft to follow Jeanotte down to help suppress ground fire, and the transport landed on the north end of the strip and rolled out slowly with all hands looking for the team. Bookie 750 landed in a storm of fire; the crew could see bullets striking the ground by them as they taxied. Not seeing the men, but seeing the enemy firing at the airplane, Jeanotte applied full power and took off. As he rolled by the team, they came out of their ditch calling to and waving at and chasing the now accelerating C-123. As the airplane moved away from them, the disheartened team ran back to their ditch on the left side of the runway, convinced they had not been seen, more pessimistic than ever. As Jeanotte got airborne, however, he banked his aircraft to the left, and the crew engineer saw the three men running back to their ditch. Jeanotte called this out over the radios and told Gatewood that he would go around and try again. But he then noticed that he did not have enough fuel to make another assault takeoff.[9] He broadcast his fuel problem and started back for Da Nang. His mission was not wasted by any means, for he had determined that the CCT was still alive and had fixed their location. He could and did brief the next crew on the position of the three men. When Jeanotte called out that he did not have enough fuel for another approach, Hillsboro called on the crew of the next airplane in the stack to go in and rescue the team. The crew did not hesitate.

THE LAST C-123 MISSION INTO KHAM DUC

Like all other aircraft at Kham Duc that day, this next C-123 was a flight diverted from a normal airlift mission. The aircraft commander was Lt Col Joe M. Jackson, the C-123 detachment commander at Da Nang for the 315 Air Commando Wing, based at Phan Rang. Jackson had earned his pilot's wings during World War II, was a jet fighter pilot during the Korean War and a U-2 pilot during the Cold War. He began the day with an unannounced flight examination. His copilot was Maj Jesse W. Campbell, called Bill, an instructor pilot and flight examiner with much valuable experience in the C-123. He had flown routinely into Khe Sanh during its darkest days. The check ride was a common measure to keep all aircrews up to professional

USAF C-123 similar to those flown by Jeanotte and Jackson on 12 May. Note the jet engines outboard of the propellers.

standards. The crew was diverted back to Da Nang at about 1400 to be briefed on their new mission. They were told about Kham Duc and what their job was: to get overhead the camp and to go in when their turn came to rescue those on the ground. All four members of the crew drew flak vests, extra ammunition for their .38 caliber pistols, and one extra M-16 rifle. The crew topped off their fuel, Campbell told Jackson the check ride was complete (and that he had passed), and they took off for Kham Duc at 1500. The crew, which was in C-123 number 543, call sign Bookie 771, arrived overhead Kham Duc at 1530. They were there an hour awaiting their turn, and they knew full well what was going on. While they waited, they drifted over the field at about 9,000 feet altitude to see if they could gain better insights by being directly overhead. When Jeanotte reported that he did not have enough fuel for another attempt, Gatewood called Jackson. He immediately pulled the throttles back to idle and told Campbell to drop the flaps to full down. Campbell replied over the radio: "Roger, going in." On the way down Jackson talked to Jeanotte about the location of the CCT. Jackson intended to taxi right up to them. In the descent he briefed the crew on their responsibilities on this assault landing and subsequent takeoff. The engineer, TSgt Edward M. Trejo, was to insure that the aircraft panel stayed set for an immediate takeoff and that jet engines, which were needed for an immediate takeoff, were never shut down. After landing he was to help the loadmaster, SSgt Manson Grubbs, pull the CCT into the airplane. Jackson made sure that Campbell knew what was expected of him, which was no

61

Alfred J. Jeanotte, Jr.

Jeanotte receiving the Air Force Cross for his actions at Kham Duc on 12 May.

Jesse W. Campbell, C-123 Flight Examiner and co-pilot on Jackson's crew for the last mission, (left) and Manson Grubbs, C-123 loadmaster on Jackson's crew (right). Campbell later received the Air Force Cross and Grubbs the Silver Star.

Edward Trejo receiving the Silver Star for his part in the Kham Duc evacuation. He was the flight engineer on Jackson's crew.

problem because Campbell had more flight time in the airplane than Jackson. The choice the crew made was to sideslip the airplane so that it would fall as rapidly as possible and present the smallest target to the enemy for the shortest period of time. To have made a standard descent with a normal downwind, base, and final approach would have made their coming known to the enemy and would have markedly reduced their chances.[10]

Jackson and Campbell worked together as a crew to accomplish this maneuver, by which the rugged C-123 can be made to descend at rates well exceeding 4,500 feet per minute. With full aileron and full opposite rudder and the throttle advanced on the engine on the top wing to take out any lift that might be developed over the horizontal stabilizer, Bookie 771 fell out of the sky. Jackson and Campbell had to worry about exceeding the flap blow-back speed, and Jackson told Trejo to be especially mindful of that. If the flaps came up at all the aircraft might overshoot, a disaster they could not afford. They planned to round out at 50 feet above the ground, 1/4 mile from the runway, and that left no margin for error: they wanted one chance and were employing an unforgiving technique that would permit just that. They dove for the runway; rounded out barely 50 feet above the ground; straightened out; landed on the extremely littered, pockmarked runway; and rolled out. Because of the crashed C-130 and CH-47 and the location of the CCT, they landed on the north end of the field and had only 2,200 feet of runway to stop in. Normally this would not have posed a problem, but Jackson could not reverse his engines; this action always shut down the two small jet engines on the C-123's wing tips, and the crew could not afford to wait for these engines to come on speed again, because they were critical for an assault takeoff.[11]

Jackson was surprised that he did not blow a tire after landing because of the sharp fragments on the runway and the holes in the asphalt surface, some of which were two feet deep. The crew was also surprised that they made it at all because they could see bullets striking all around them and could hear the sound of the enemy guns and mortars above the roar of their four engines. While the crew was on the ground they could actually see tracer fire pass beneath the airplane. After roll out the crew saw the CCT come out of a ditch and run for the airplane, the two enlisted men firing their M-16s at the enemy all the way. Jackson was turning the airplane to go out to the north, over the same end of the runway he had landed on. He could see bullets striking the runway in front of and behind the men running from the ditch about 100 feet from the airplane. As Grubbs and Trejo pulled the three men inside the airplane, Jackson heard Campbell call: "Look out!" Down the runway, straight at them, came a 122 mm rocket. This weapon, which has a normal range of six to eight miles, had apparently been fired at them from the ridge to the immediate north of the runway. It struck short of the C-123, bounced, spun around several times and skidded to a stop a few feet in front of the nosewheel—and the warhead failed to explode. Jackson used nosewheel steering to taxi gingerly around the rocket, now bent in a horseshoe shape; pushed the throttles to the firewall; ran up the jets; and pulled the C-123 off the asphalt runway in about 1,100 feet. He took his passengers to Da Nang.

Joe M. Jackson
In this photo Jackson is wearing the Medal of Honor he was presented for his heroism at Kham Duc on 12 May. This was Jackson's third war, if one does not count his U-2 missions during the Cold War. He became an Army Air Forces pilot during World War II, flew more than 100 jet fighter missions during the Korean War and also more than a hundred missions during the Viet Nam War. Jackson was the only airlift crewmember to win a Medal of Honor during the Viet Nam War.

Bookie 771 had been on the ground less than a full minute, but it was probably the longest fraction of a minute in the CCT's and aircrew's lives. While the rescue proceeded, no one above talked on the radios, and a most interested audience kept its silence, hoped for the best, and held its breath. Despite the fact that the enemy had fired at Bookie 771 while it was descending, while it was on the runway, and also on takeoff, when the crew got out at Da Nang to count bullet holes, there were none.[12]

To the CCT and aircrew it was a miraculous escape, and like so much that happened at Kham Duc on 12 May 1968—Mother's Day that year—the final rescue, like all the others, can be attributed to the skill, tenacity, and courage of the American aircrew.

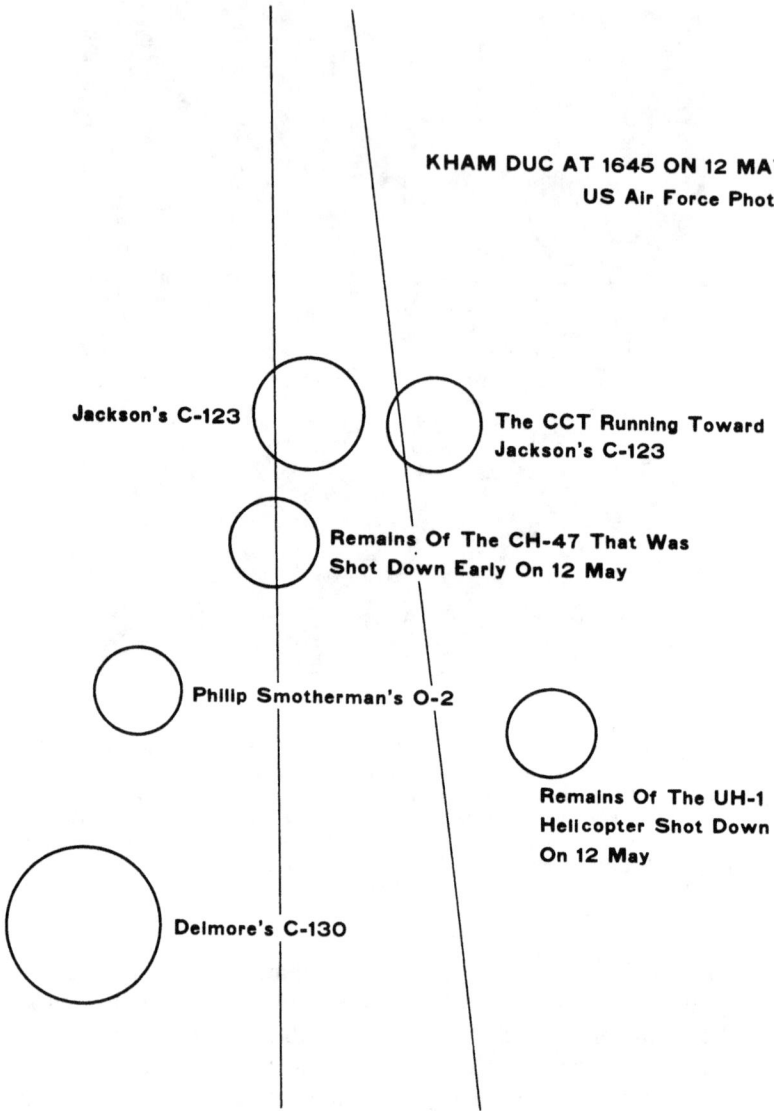

KHAM DUC AT 1645 ON 12 MAY

US Air Force Photo

Jackson's C-123

The CCT Running Toward
Jackson's C-123

Remains Of The CH-47 That Was
Shot Down Early On 12 May

Philip Smotherman's O-2

Remains Of The UH-1
Helicopter Shot Down
On 12 May

Delmore's C-130

Kham Duc at 1645 on 12 May.

Appendix A

Glossary of Terms and Abbreviations

A-1E	US, single-engine, piston-driven fighter/bomber
A-4D	Marine, single-engine, jet attack fighter
AB	Air Base
ABCCC	Airborne Battlefield Command and Control Center
AC-47	USAF, twin-engine, piston-driven light transport modified to serve as a gunship
AFSHRC	Albert F. Simpson Historical Research Center
ALCC	Airlift Control Center
Al	Alabama
ALCE	Airlift Control Element
AFB	Air Force Base
AK-47	Soviet-designed, semi-automatic infantry rifle
ALO	Air Liaison Officer
A Team	US Army Special Forces basic advisory unit
B-52	USAF, eight-engine, jet heavy bomber
BGen	Brigadier General
C-7A	USAF, twin-engine, piston-driven, lightweight, small-capacity, short takeoff-and-landing transport
C-47	USAF, twin-engine, piston-driven, light transport
C-123	USAF, four-engine (two piston, two jet) medium-capacity, short-takeoff-and-landing transport (Not all C-123s were equipped with the two jet engines, but those mentioned in this monograph were.) The C-123 had much more capacity than the C-7A but less than the C-130.
C-130	USAF, four-engine, turbo-prop medium-capacity transport.
Capt	Captain
CBU	Clustered Bomb Units
CCT	Combat Control Team
CDS	Container Delivery System
CG	Commanding General
CH-46	Marine, twin-engine, large-capacity, transport helicopter
CH-47	Army, twin-engine, large-capacity, transport helicopter
Charlie	Viet Cong
CHECO	Contemporary Historical Examination of Current Operations

CIDG	Civilian Irregular Defense Group
COC	Combat Operations Center
Col	Colonel
COMUSMACV	Commander, US Military Assistance Command, Vietnam
F-4	USAF twin-engine, two-place jet fighter/bomber
F-5	Twin-engine light fighter/bomber, built by the US and flown by the Vietnamese air force
F-100	USAF single-engine, jet attack fighter
F-105	USAF single-engine, jet attack fighter
DISUM	Daily Intelligence Summary
FAC	Forward Air Controller
FM	Frequency Modulation
FOB	Forward Operating Base
G-3	Army Operations
Gen	General
Grand SLAM	Nickname for an all-forces heavy firepower assault north of the demilitarized zone. SLAM stands for seek, locate, annihiliate and monitor.
Ha	Hawaii
HAFB	Hickam Air Force Base
Hilda	Call sign for 834 Air Division ALCC
Hillsboro	Call sign for ABCCC overhead Kham Duc on 12 May 1968
HQ	Headquarters
I Corps	South Vietnam's northernmost military district
I DASC	I Corps Direct Air Support Center (An USAF organization based at Da Nang AB.)
JN	Jet Navigation chart
KC 135	USAF four-engine, jet tanker
Lt Col	Lieutenant Colonel
Lt Gen	Lieutenant General
Ltr	Letter
LZ	Landing Zone
M-16	US-manufactured, semi-automatic infantry rifle
MACV	Military Assistance Command, Vietnam
MAFB	Maxwell Air Force Base
Maj	Major
0-1	USAF single-engine, piston-driven light observation airplane
0-2	USAF two-engine, piston-driven light observation aircraft (one engine was a pusher and one was a tractor)
PACAF	Pacific Air Forces
SEA	Southeast Asia
Slick	Nickname for an unarmed (except for light defensive armament) helicopter

Spad	Nickname and sometimes call sign for A-1E airplanes
Spooky	Nickname and call sign for AC-47 gunship aircraft
SSgt	Staff Sergeant
TAW	Tactical Airlift Wing
TACC	Tactical Air Control Center
TACP	Tactical Air Control Party
TOC	Tactical Operations Center
TSgt	Technical Sergeant
UH-1C	Army single-engine armed attack helicopter
UH-1N	Army single-engine light helicopter
UHF	Ultra High Frequency
US	United States
USAF	United States Air Force
VHF	Very High Frequency
7th Air Force (7 AF)	Single manager for airpower in Southeast Asia
834th Air Division (834 AD)	Manager for all airlift in Southeast Asia

Appendix B

South Vietnam

Appendix C

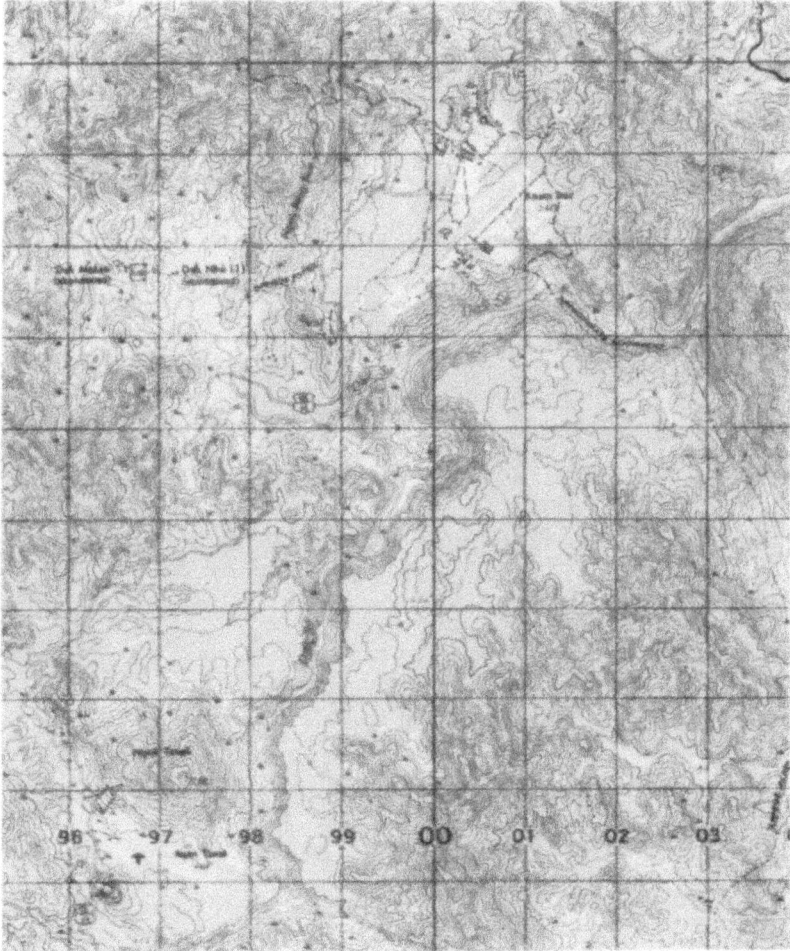

Notes on Chapter I

1. Bernard C. Nalty, *Airpower and the Fight for Khe Sanh,* Washington, DC, Office of Air Force History, 1973, pp. 28-31, 103-105.

2. Letter (Ltr), Peter H. Jackson to author, undated [November 1977]. This letter and all others received by the author will be deposited in the Albert F. Simpson Historical Research Center (AFSHRC) at Maxwell AFB (MAFB), Alabama (Al). The author of this monograph was a navigator on a C-130 that landed at Kham Duc in late April 1968 during the rebuilding phase. The description of the terrain is his, but the vulnerability of the site was obvious to Jackson (see his letter) and to the author's colleagues who flew into Kham Duc.

3. Daniel F. Schungel, "After Action Report Battle of Kham Duc," 31 May 1968, AFSHRC, MAFB, Al. This document, as with nearly all those in the monograph, is on microfilm as supporting documents for various Project CHECO reports (CHECO; CONTEMPORARY HISTORICAL EXAMINATION OF CURRENT OPERATIONS); see microfilm 02CH/29/2/4 & Sup.

4. Alfred G. Hutchins, "Dissemination of Threat Information on Kham Duc Special Forces Camp," 13 May 1968, AFSHRC, MAFB, Al. This letter contains three attachments specifying the threat to Kham Duc; see microfilm 02CH/29/2/4 & Sup.

5. Kenneth Sams and A. W. Thompson, "Kham Duc," Hickam AFB (HAFB), Hawaii (Ha), Headquarters, Pacific Air Forces (PACAF), 8 July 1968, pp. 5, 6. This is a CHECO report and can be found at AFSHRC. See also Schungel, "After Action Report Battle of Kham Duc."

6. Sams and Thompson, "Kham Duc," pp. 5, 6, and the paraphrased press interview of BGen J. E. Glick et al., undated AFSHRC, MAFB, Al. On microfilm 02CH/29/2/4 & Sup. See also Cecil Brownlow, "Coordinated Effort Saves Force," *Aviation Week & Space Technology,* Volume 89, Number 11, September 9, 1968, pp. 92-98.

7. Jackson Letter.

8. Glick, et al. interview; and Schungel, "After Action Report."

9. Sams and Thompson, "Kham Duc," pp. 5, 6, and Daniel F. Schungel, "After Action Report Ngoc Tavak FOB," 16 May 1968, AFSHRC, MAFB, Al. On microfilm 02CH/29/2/4 & Sup. This report is a part of the previously cited "Kham Duc After Action Report." See also undated statement by William F. Hull, AFSHRC, MAFB, Al. On microfilm 02 CH/29/2/4 & Sup. Hull's statement is support for the two previously cited after action reports and is appended to them.

10. Sams and Thompson, "Kham Duc," pp. 5, 6, and Daniel F. Schungel, "After Action Report Ngoc Tavak FOB," 16 May 1968, AFSHRC, MAFB, Al. On microfilm 02CH/29/2/4 & Sup. This report is a part of the previously cited "Kham Duc After Action Report." See also undated statement by William F. Hull, AFSHRC, MAFB, Al. On microfilm 02 CH/29/2/4 & Sup. Hull's statement is support for the two previously cited after action reports and is appended to them.

11. Sams and Thompson, "Kham Duc," pp. 5, 6, and Daniel F. Schungel, "After Action Report Ngoc Tavak FOB," 16 May 1968, AFSHRC, MAFB, Al. On microfilm 02CH/29/2/4 & Sup. This report is a part of the previously cited "Kham Duc After Action Report." See also undated statement by William F. Hull, AFSHRC, MAFB, Al. On microfilm 02 CH/29/2/4 & Sup. Hull's statement is support for the two previously cited after action reports and is appended to them. See also undated statement of Capt Eugene Edward Makowski, AFSHRC, MAFB, Al. See microfilm 02CH/29/2/4 & Sup. Makowski's statement is appended to the two previously cited after action reports; he was the on-scene commander of the CIDG forces on 10 May at Ngoc Tavak. See also "TACC Intel Journal- Opened 10 May 1968," AFSHRC, MAFB, Al. On microfilm 02CH/29/2/4 & Sup. TACC means Tactical Air Control Center.

12. Sams and Thompson, "Kham Duc," and Schungel, "After Action Report Ngoc Tavak FOB." See also Makowski statement.

13. Sams and Thompson, "Kham Duc," and Schungel, "After Action Report Ngoc Tavak FOB." See also Makowski statement; Hull statement.

14. Message from Commanding General III MAF to COMUSMACV, "Action At Kham Duc 12 May 1968," AFSHRC, MAFB, Al. On microfilm 02CH/29/2/4 & Sup. This message is from Lt Gen Robert E. Cushman to Gen William C. Westmoreland, Commander United States Military Assistance Command, Vietnam.

15. Sams and Thompson, "Kham Duc," pp. 32-33.

16. Ibid., pp. 5, 6. See also History and Museum's Division, *The Marines in Vietnam, 1954-1973, An Anthology and Annotated Bibliography,* Washington, DC, Headquarters US Marine Corps, 1974, p. 107. See William C. Westmoreland, *A Solider Reports,* New York, Doubleday and Co., 1976, p. 360. See also William C. Westmoreland, *Report on Operations in South Vietnam January 1964-June 1968.* Section II of *Report on the War in Vietnam (As of 30 June 1968),* Washington, DC, 1968, pp. 167, 168.

17. Undated statement by James Duncan and undated statement by James R. Aydock, AFSHRC, MAFB, Al. See microfilm 02CH/29/2/4 & Sup. See also Schungel, "After Action Report Kham Duc." Both of the former statements are appended to the latter report.

18. Schungel, "After Action Report Kham Duc." See also I DASC DISUM # 12-68, AFSHRC, MAFB, Al. On microfilm 02CH/29/2/4 & Sup. I DASC means I Corps Direct Air Support Center, and DISUM means daily intelligence summary.

19. Sams and Thompson, "Kham Duc," pp. 32, 33.

20. Schungel, "After Action Report Kham Duc." See Sams and Thompson, "Kham Duc," Document 6. On microfilm 02CH/29/2/4 & Sup. Document 6 is a little difficult to find; it is a compilation of messages that provide a running commentary on the battles at Ngoc Tavak and Kham Duc. It is without a title but can be found on the microfilm reel marked with a penciled "6" with a circle around it. Its first entry is "10 May 68, 0608." It will be listed hereafter as "Document 6."

21. Glick, et al. interview. See also Schungel, "After Action Report Kham Duc." See undated statement by Robert Henderson, AFSHRC, MAFB, Al. On microfilm 02CH/29/2/4 & Sup. Henderson's statement is appended to Schungel's after action report.

22. Undated statement by Richard F. Campbell, AFSHRC, MAFB, Al. On microfilm 02CH/29/2/4 & Sup. Campbell's statement is also part of Schungel's after action report.

23. Henderson statement.

24. Undated statement by Eugene Bernhart, AFSHRC, MAFB, Al. On microfilm 02CH/29/2/4 & Sup. Bernhart's statement is appended to Schungel's after action report.

25. Telephone interview, author with Claude H. Turner, 25 October 1977.

26. Duncan statement. See also Brownlow, "Coordinated Effort."

27. Duncan statement.

28. Aydock statement.

29. Duncan statement. See also Glick, et al. interview.

30. Kenneth Sams, "The Air War in Vietnam 1968-1969," HAFB, Ha., PACAF, 1 April 1970, p. 34. This can be found at AFSHRC. See Glick, et al. interview. See also Sams and Thompson, "Kham Duc," p. 2.

31. Sams and Thompson, "Kham Duc," p. 2.

32. Schungel, "After Action Report Kham Duc."

Notes on Chapter II

1. Sams and Thompson, "Kham Duc," p. 1. See also Brownlow, "Coordinated Effort." pp. 92-98. Sams and Thompson write that there were 110 Marine CH-46 sorties. I believe this number is much too high. They report that Army CH-47s carried out more evacuees than the Marines, and if each CH-46 carried out its load of nine, then the Marines would have carried out close to 1,000. It is known that the Air Force took out more than 665 and that the Marines and Army took out slightly more than that; therefore the figure of 110 is unreliable. Sams and Thompson got their figure from Lt Gen Cushman's message to Gen Westmoreland, and that figure is repeated in Brownlow's article. Taking the number of statements provided by Marine pilots and knowing that the Marines rescued around 300 people, I estimate the number of sorties to be in the low 30s.

2. Telephone interview, author with Philip R. Smotherman, 26 Oct 1977.

3. Statement by S. T. Summerman, 28 May 1968. See also statement by Wesley R. Marks, 28 May 1968, AFSHRC, MAFB, Al. See microfilm 02CH/29/2/4 & Sup for both statements.

4. Statements by James L. Busby and Ernest M. Wood, both 28 May 1968, AFSHRC, MAFB, Al. On microfilm 02CH/29/2/4 & Sup for both statements.

5. This information came from an unidentified voice on a series of cassette tapes at AFSHRC, MAFB, Al. These tapes were donated to AFSHRC by Philip R. Smotherman, who was a FAC on 12 May overhead and on the ground at Kham Duc. He enters the narrative below. Smotherman secured these taped statements and saved them for nearly a decade. The tapes can be heard (they have not been transcribed, and there are no plans at present for transcribing them) at AFSHRC. The call number of the tapes is #K 239.0512, and this particular segment is on side 1 of tape 1. The gunship pilots identified themselves as being from Chu Lai. The "Slick" pilot was named Mr. Fitzsimmons (no other names). Unfortunately we do not know the name of the pilot rescued by Fitzsimmons since not even his unit history names him. Identifying fighter pilots involved in the evacuation has proved to be impossible within the time limits of the project. Not a single fighter pilot or crew is identified in any of the unit histories of all the units involved, and most of the unit histories do not even mention having crews at Kham Duc that day.

6. Tape recording #K 239.0512, side 1 tape 2, AFSHRC, MAFB, Al. Again, no names mentioned.

7. Sams and Thompson, "Kham Duc," pp. 13, 14.

8. See Schungel, "After Action Report Kham Duc," for a critique of the lack of coordination caused by lack of radio commonality. The Special

Forces and Col Nelson found the "control of tactical air and coordination of tactical air strikes" to be a "critical problem" all day. Nelson, who believed he knew the best targets, wanted to have some input into the targets struck by the fighter pilot, but was unable to talk to the air crews. The lack of FM radios in the fighters was a frustration, but it is doubtful that the Air Force would want the ground element leader talking directly to its fighter crews.

9. Wood and Summerman statements. See also Sams and Thompson, "Kham Duc," pp. 27, 28-30.

10. Statement by William F. Tinnan, 28 May 1968, AFSHRC, MAFB, Al. On microfilm 02CH/29/2/4 & Sup.

11. Marks statement.

12. Statement by Paul H. Moody, 28 May 1968, AFSHRC, MAFB, Al. On microfilm 02CH/29/2/4 & Sup.

Notes on Chapter III

1. Ltr ALO to G-3, Subject: Kham Duc Action, 11 and 12 May 1968, dated 14 May 1968, AFSHRC, MAFB, Al. See microfilm 02CH/29/2/4 & Sup. G-3 is Army Operations.

2. Nalty, pp. 72, 74, 76.

3. Chronological Order of Events, Kham Duc Special Forces Camp, 12 May 1968, AFSHRC, MAFB, Al. See microfilm 02CH/29/2/4 & Sup. The times of specific events in this chronology do not always agree with other evidence, but the sequence is more important than the timing. In some cases the times used in my manuscript differ from the chronology when in the author's judgment the documents cited are more accurate. When times are used that disagree with the chronology, it is because an eyewitness recorded the time and usually more than one eyewitness differs from the chronology. This chronology was compiled for Gen Momyer on 14 May. It is an amalgam of interviews with TACC personnel (who got their information always after the fact and usually second or third hand) and logs from the TACC and the TACC senior duty officer log book.

4. Telephone interview of Robert Gatewood, 26 October 1977. Gatewood did not believe that the coordination between ABCCC and FACs and fighters was as good as it could have been, but he thinks it was adequate

given the nature of the emergency. One FAC, James Gibler, thought the ABCCC got in the way (telephone interview with Gibler, 10 November 1977). But the FAC longest on the scene, Philip Smotherman, thought the ABCCC performed "outstandingly," acting as a "mini-DASC." Smotherman telephone interview 26 October 1977.

5. Smotherman telephone interview.

6. Tape recording #K 239.0512, side 1, tape 1. The voice is unidentified, but it is probably Willard C. Johnson's.

7. Sams and Thompson, "Kham Duc," pp. 32-33.

8. Log, I Corps DASC, AFSHRC, MAFB, AL. On microfilm 02CH/29/2/4 & Sup.

9. Chronological Order of Events.

10. Ibid.

11. Sams and Thompson, "Kham Duc," pp. 7, 8. See Chronological Order of Events. See also Document 6.

12. Updated Statement by Herbert J. Spier, AFSHRC, MAFB, Al. See microfilm 02CH/29/2/4 & Sup.

13. Tape #K 239.0512, side 1, tape 2.

14. Sams and Thompson, "Kham Duc," p. 5. See statement by Reese B. Black, 16 May 1968, AFSHRC, MAFB, Al. On microfilm 02CH/29/2/4 & Sup.

15. Sams and Thompson, "Kham Duc," pp. 22-25. See statements by Richard J. Smith, 16 May 1968 and Jack Anderson, 29 May 1968, both AFSHRC, MAFB, Al. On microfilm 02CH/29/2/4 & Sup for both statements.

16. Sams and Thompson, "Kham Duc," pp. 22-25. See statements by Richard J. Smith, 16 May 1968 and Jack Anderson, 29 May 1968, both AFSHRC, MAFB, Al. On microfilm 02CH/29/2/4 & Sup for both statements. See interview author with Walter Hersman at MAFB, Al., 21 December 1977. Hersman was overhead Kham Duc on 12 May in an F-100. See also statement by Richard J. Smith, 16 May 1968, AFSHRC, MAFB, Al. On microfilm 02CH/29/2/4 & Sup.

17. Statement by Richard P. Schuman, 28 May 1968, AFSHRC, MAFB, Al. On microfilm 02CH/29/2/4 & Sup.

18. Tape #K 239.0512, side 2, tape 2.

19. Ibid. See statement by Philip R. Smotherman, 29 May 1968, AFSHRC, MAFB, Al. On microfilm 02CH/29/2/4 & Sup.

20. Statement by James Gibler, 18 May 1968, AFSHRC, MAFB, Al. On microfilm 02/CH/29/2/4 & Sup. See Sams and Thompson, "Kham Duc," pp. 22-25.

21. Tape #K 239.0512, side 2, tape 2.

22. Sams and Thompson, "Kham Duc," pp. 22–25; See also Schungel, "After Action Report Kham Duc."

23. Tape #K 239.0512, side 2, tape 2.

24. Statement by James M. Mead, 16 May 1968, AFSHRC, MAFB, Al. On microfilm 02/CH/29/2/4 & Sup.

25. Smith statement.

26. Ibid. See also statement by James M. Fogle, 16 May 1968, AFSHRC, MAFB, Al. On microfilm 02CH/29/2/4 & Sup.

27. Fogle and Mead statements.

28. Brownlow, "Coordinated Effort." pp. 92-98.

29. Fogle and Mead statements.

Notes on Chapter IV

1. Document 6. See also Chronological Order of Events.

2. Statement by Charles Herrington, 17 May 1968, AFSHRC, MAFB, Al. On microfilm 02CH/29/2/4 & Sup.

3. Sams and Thompson, "Kham Duc," pp. 10, 11.

4. Chronological Order of Events.

5. Ibid.

6. Sams and Thompson, "Kham Duc," pp. 15, 16. See statement by Dave C. Hearell, 17 May 1968. On microfilm 02CH/29/2/4 & Sup.

7. Jackson letter.

8. Schungel, "After Action Report Kham Duc."

9. Gary H. Saban, "History of the 374th Tactical Airlift Wing, 1 July-31 October 1968," pp. 77-82. This can be found at AFSHRC.

10. Brownlow, "Coordinated Effort," pp. 92-98. See letter, Morton Freedman to author, 30 October 1977. See also Bob Cutts, "On a Wing and a Prayer," *Pacific Stars and Stripes,* 11 August 1968, pp. A3-A6.

11. Sams and Thompson, "Kham Duc," p. 14.

12. Ibid., pp. 17-19.

13. Ibid.

14. "History of the 463 Tactical Airlift Wing, April-June 1968," pp. 21-23. This can be found at AFSHRC.

15. Tape #239.0512, side 2, tape 1. This is Spier talking.

16. Ted R. Sturm, "The Lucky Duc," *Airman,* Volume 14, Number 9, October 1970, pp. 26-29.

17. Interview of John McCall by Ray Bowers, undated. This interview will be deposited at AFSHRC.

18. Saban. See also Sams and Thompson, "Kham Duc," pp. 17-19. See Debrief of Aircrews from Kham Duc, AFSHRC, MAFB, Al. On microfilm 02CH/29/2/4 & Sup.

19. Debrief of Aircrews. See also Sams and Thompson, "Kham Duc," pp. 17-19.

20. Telephone interview of James L. Wallace by Ray Bowers, 3 April 1972. This interview will be deposited at AFSHRC. See also tape #K239.0512, side 2, tape 2, Smotherman speaking.

21. Kham Duc Summary Sheet, AFSHRC, MAFB, Al. On microfilm 02CH/29/2/4 & Sup. See Sams and Thompson, "Kham Duc," pp. 17-19.

22. Chronological Order of Events. See also Brownlow, "Coordinated Effort." pp. 92-98. See Freedman letter. See telephone interview, author with Burl McLaughlin, 22 January 1978. Worse yet, there was another airplane in the pattern with another CCT onboard. This C-130 was piloted by Maj Norman Jensen of the 463 TAW. Jensen was on temporary duty to Tan Son Nhut AB at Saigon and permanently assigned to Mactan AB. He was in the landing pattern when called by Hilda to take the CCT back to base. Jensen telephone interview by author, 3 Nov 1977. See also letter Paul E. Dahle to Ray Bowers, 25 November 1972. Dahle was Jensen's navigator.

Notes on Chapter V

1. According to an undated statement by Richard F. Campbell, the major in command of the CCT came to the A Team "right after the initial mortar rounds began to fall" and said that he wanted his men evacuated. See microfilm 02CH/29/2/4 & Sup for Campbell statement, AFSHRC, MAFB, AL.

2. Cutts, "On a Wing and a Prayer." See also Mission Report for Tailpipe Delta, AFSHRC, MAFB, Al. On microfilm 02CH/29/2/4 & Sup.

3. Brownlow, "Coordinated Effort," pp. 92-98. See also letter, Edward Carr to author, undated [November 1977]. Carr was Van Cleeff's navigator. He confirmed to this author that the crew picked up no one. He was on the ramp at the rear of the airplane taking motion pictures while the crew awaited the return of the CCT.

4. Telephone interview of Carr by author, 3 November 1977. Interview of Jan Van Cleeff by author, 22 May 1978.

5. Ltr Carr to Gropman; see also Ltr Gatewood to 834AD Commander, AFSHRC, MAFB, AL. On microfilm 02CH/29/2/4 & Sup.

6. Freedman letter. See also "Mission Report for Tailpipe Delta."

7. Cutts, "On a Wing and a Prayer."

8. "History of 315 Air Commando Wing, April-June 1968," Tab 17, statement by TSgt Morton J. Freedman, attested to by Maj Ira Allen. This can be found at AFSHRC. See also Freedman letter. There are numerous minor discrepancies in the various accounts of the final rescue. Freedman in his statement to Allen said that men were picked up on Van Cleeff's C-130, and Gatewood wrote the same thing to McLaughlin. But Carr denies this, and he was with the airplane all the way out and back to Cam Ranh Bay. Also, Smotherman wanted to be the last to leave Kham Duc, and in all the conversations and correspondence he never mentioned anybody leaving the airplane he boarded. He and Henderson were determined to be the last on the ground and would not have permitted anybody to run off the C-130 ramp into the smoke and fire.

9. Telephone interview of Alfred Jeanotte, Jr., by author 5 November 1977. See also Ltr Gatewood to Commander 834AD. See CCT Mission Report for Tailpipe Delta. See Sams and Thompson, "Kham Duc," pp. 17-19.

10. Flint Du Pre, "Rescue at a Place Called Kham Duc," *Air Force Magazine,* Volume 52, Number 3 March 1969, pp. 98-100. See also Ted R. Sturm, "Flight Check to Glory," *Airman,* Volume XIII, Number 9,

September 1969, pp. 52-54. See Oral History Interview of Col Joe M. Jackson by Hugh N.Ahmann,7 and 13 October 1971, AFSHRC, MAFB, Al. See statement by Joe M. Jackson, 18 May 1968, AFSHRC, MAFB, Al. See microfilm 02CH./29/2/4 & Sup.

11. Flint Du Pre, "Rescue at a Place Called Kham Duc," *Air Force Magazine,* Volume 52, Number 3 March 1969, pp. 98-100. See also Ted R. Sturm, "Flight Check to Glory," *Airman,* Volume XIII, Number 9, September 1969, pp. 52-54. See Oral History Interview of Col Joe M. Jackson by Hugh N. Ahmann, 7 and 13 October 1971, AFSHRC, MAFB, Al. See microfilm 02CH/29/2/4 & Sup. Telephone interview of Jesse W. Campbell by author, 3 November 1977. See citation to accompany the award of the Air Force Cross to Jesse W. Campbell. This will be deposited at AFSHRC.

12. Flint Du Pre, "Rescue at a Place Called Kham Duc," *Air Force Magazine,* Volume 52, Number 3 March 1969, pp. 98-100. See also Ted R. Sturm, "Flight Check to Glory," *Airman,* Volume XIII, Number 9, September 1969, pp. 52-54. See Oral History Interview of Col Joe M. Jackson by Hugh N. Ahmann, 7 and 13 October 1972, AFSHRC, MAFB, AL. See statement by Joe M. Jackson, 18 May 1968, AFSHRC, MAFB, Al. See microfilm 02CH/29/2/4 & Sup.
the Medal of Honor to Joe M. Jackson and the supporting data for same, *Congressional Record: Senate,* 1969, pp. 1043-1044. See letter Jackson to author, undated [November 1977].

Bibliography

Manuscript Collection

Microfilm 02CH/29/2/4 & Sup, AFSHRC, MAFB, Al. This previously classified body of documents forms the spine of this monograph. Kenneth Sams and A. E. Thompson collected them for their report on Kham Duc.

Books

Nalty, Bernard C. *Air Power and the Fight for Khe Sanh*. Washington: GPO (Office of Air Force History), 1973.

Westmoreland, William C. *A Soldier Reports*. New York: Doubleday and Co., 1976.

Periodicals

Brownlow, Cecil. "Coordinated Effort Saves Force." *Aviation Week and Space Technology*, 89: 92-98.

Cutts, Bob. "On a Wing and a Prayer," *Pacific Stars and Stripes*, 11 August 1968, pp. A-3 and A-6.

DuPre, Flint. "Rescue at a Place called Kham Duc," *Air Force Magazine*, 52: 98-100.

Sturm, Ted R. "Flight Check to Glory," *Airman*, Volume XIII, Number 9, 52-54.

_____ , "The Lucky Duc," *Airman*, Volume XIV, Number 9, October 1970, 26-29.

Unpublished Reports

McLaughlin, Burl W. "End of Tour Report." This can be found at AFSHRC.

Saban, Gary H. "History of 374th Tactical Airlift Wing, 1 July-31 October 1968." This can be found at AFSHRC.

Sams, Kenneth and Thompson, A. W. "Kham Duc." A Project CHECO Report, HQ PACAF, Directorate of Tactical Evaluation, CHECO Division, HAFB, Ha. This can be found at AFSHRC.

Sams, et al. "The Air War in Viet Nam, 1968-1969." A Project CHECO Report, HQ PACAF, Directorate of Tactical Evaluation, CHECO Division, HAFB, Ha. This can be found at AFSHRC.

Westmoreland, William C. "Report on the War in Vietnam, Section II, Report on Operations in South Viet Nam January 1964-June 1968."

Washington, GPO. This can be found at MAFB in the Air University Library.

'The Marines in Vietnam, 1954-1973, An Anthology and Annotated Bibliography." History and Museums Division, Headquarters US Marine Corps, Washington, DC, 1974. This can be found at MAFB in the Air University Library.

"History of 314th Air Commando Wing, April-June 1968.". This can be found at AFSHRC.

Interviews

Campbell, Jesse W. by author, telecon, 3 November 1977.

Carr, Edward G. by author, telecon, 3 November 1977.

Jackson, Joe M. by Hugh N. Ahmann, 7, 13 October 1971. This can be found at AFSHRC.

Jackson, Joe M. by author, November, December 1977, May 1978.

Jeanotte, Alfred J., Jr. by author, telecon, 5 November 1977.

Jensen, Norman K. by author, telecon, 3 November 1977.

McLaughlin, Burl W. by author, telecon, 22 January 1978.

Niblack, Emmet A. by Ray Bowers, 3 May 1972. This can be found at AFSHRC.

Smotherman, Philip R. by author, telecon, 26 October 1977.

Turner, Claude H. by author, telecon, 25 October 1977.

Van Cleeff, Jay. by author, 22 May 1978.

Award Citations

Citation to accompany Willian Boyd's Air Force Cross. This will be deposited at AFSHRC.

Citation to accompany Jesse W. Campbell's Air Force Cross. This will be deposited at AFSHRC.

Citation to accompany Joe M. Jackson's Medal of Honor with supporting data, *Congressional Record, Senate,* 1969, pp. 1043-1044.

Citation to accompany Alfred J. Jeanotte, Jr.'s Air Force Cross. This will be deposited at AFSHRC.

Tape

Cassette tape recording call number #K 239.0512, AFSHRC, MAFB, Al.

Letters

Carr, Edward to author, undated [November 1977]. This will be deposited at AFSHRC.

_____ . undated [February 1978]. This will be deposited at AFSHRC.

Dahle, Paul E. to Ray Bowers, 25 November 1972. This will be deposited at AFSHRC.

Freedman, Morton to author, 30 October 1977. This will be deposited at AFSHRC.

Gatewood, Robert M. to author, undated [October 1977]. This will be deposited at AFSHRC.

Jackson, Peter H. to author, undated [November 1977]. This will be deposited at AFSHRC.

www.ingramcontent.com/pod-product-compliance
Lightning Source LLC
LaVergne TN
LVHW021541080426
835509LV00019B/2763